MANAGERS AND CORPORATE SOCIAL POLICY

Also by Brian Harvey
ENVIRONMENT AND SOCIETY: An Introductory
Analysis (*with John Hallett*)

Also by Barry Wilkinson
THE SHOPFLOOR POLITICS OF NEW TECHNOLOGY

Managers and Corporate Social Policy

Private Solutions to Public Problems?

Brian Harvey, Stephen Smith
and Barry Wilkinson

M

658.4
H 341

First published 1984 by
THE MACMILLAN PRESS LTD
London and Basingstoke
Companies and representatives
throughout the world

Typeset by
Wessex Typesetters Ltd
Frome, Somerset
Printed in Hong Kong

British Library Cataloguing in Publication Data
Harvey, Brian
Managers and corporate social policy.
1. Industry – Social aspects
I. Title   II. Smith, Stephen
III. Wilkinson, Barry
658.4'08   HD60
ISBN 0–333–36427–9

Contents

Preface

This book is about managers, with the contemporary relationship between the business enterprise and society forming the broad context within which it is set. *Managers and Corporate Social Policy: Private Solutions to Public Problems?* thus refers to the role of free enterprise in today's society. In Britain this means that discussion will take place against the background of an evolved *welfare state* in which the virtues of free enterprise are currently being vigorously re-emphasised. This is also linked to the re-emergence over the last ten years of the concept of corporate social responsibility.

These issues form the background to the research upon which this book is based, but it approaches them from a practical rather than grandly theoretical viewpoint. The two-year research project, funded by the Social Science Research Council, focused on individual firms, and more especially their managements. The central questions it posed were as follows. Does corporate social responsibility exist in observed managerial practice? In addition to the pursuit of commercial goals, are firms involved in providing private solutions to public problems, perhaps in the fields of redundancy, the quality of working life, equal opportunity or environmental pollution? How do managers perceive the role of their business enterprise in society? Do they feel capable of accepting social responsibilities, or perhaps some rather than others? What appear to be their motivations, both when they are and when they are not involved? What might be the implications of these findings for any effective future extension of the role of business in the provision of private solutions to public problems?

Chapter 1 outlines the background to the debate on the social role of the corporation. This centres on questions of the extent of corporate power and its linkage to *public* goals, in effect the legitimacy of the large private corporation in a democratic society. In the United States especially, the debate on corporate social responsibility has embraced these issues.

The second chapter focuses on managers. The *managerialist thesis* sees a divorce of ownership from management control and ascribes managers discretion which could result in a broadening of corporate objectives. We review the managerialist thesis and pose the question – are managers 'good goldfish', visible and responsive to the outside world?

The core of the book has been based on two years' intensive research of managers at work in four Midlands manufacturing firms. (The theory and methods of the research are described in the Appendix.) The case studies which thus form Chapters 3–6 show how some of the social policies of the four firms are managed. Each chapter details one company on the basis of the accounts offered mainly by managers and directors. The individual character of each firm's organisational culture is explained and linked to the way managers handle social policy issues such as black labour, local and national external relations, supplier relations, new technology, small-business promotion and environmental impact.

The first three cases describe management who 'treat the outside world like the weather', and accept only a limited competence for managing social policy issues. The fourth case, however, presents a radically different managerial culture, where managers have sought to extend their competence well beyond what may be the UK norm represented by the other cases.

The case studies are presented as far as possible without comment. Chapter 7 therefore draws together their themes and issues, and provides a comparative *political* analysis of the differences between the firms in their handling of the employment of black labour, the introduction of new technology, and local and national external relations.

Chapter 8 is devoted to the central theme of the book, *managers* and corporate social policy. It explores the broad limits and nature of corporate social responsibility, as perceived and acted upon by managers themselves in the four case-study firms. The motivations which appear to underpin corporate social policies are summarised under headings such as 'Response to direct pressures and threats', 'Commercial rationales', 'Advertising and marketing', 'External and internal ideology'. The chapter then concludes by considering the policy implications of the research. It asks: are there dangers (for both parties) in companies attempting to manage the *public interest*? Should managers be able to make social policy assessments independently of corporate interests, and would they require alternative bases of allegiance such as effective professional organisations? What might the current reassertion of the role of *private solutions to public problems* mean for British managers?

In writing this book, we wish to acknowledge the patient and willing cooperation of our respondents in the four participating companies; the essential contribution of Lesley Thomas, the project's secretary; the financial support of the Social Science Research Council; and the 'home' provided for the research team by the University of Nottingham.

1 Private Solutions to Public Problems?

The founding fathers of the great cities of Britain not only built their factories. They also created a community around them to house their labour force. They took out their profits but put back amenities, schools and parks into an area in which they too lived close at hand.

. . . I have set myself the task of helping to reverse the drift away from partnership between local authorities and local business communities. I want to engender the belief that if the private sector takes on a more positive, assertive role in local affairs, the benefits to the community will be enormous.

(Speech by the then Secretary of
State for the Environment,
Michael Heseltine)[1]

Such a reassertion of the constructive social role of free enterprise, in this case the responsibilities of major firms to their local communities, can be seen as part of the more general claim currently being made in Britain and the United States for the recognition of the effectiveness of the market system. It should also be linked to the re-emergence over the past ten years of the concept of corporate social responsibility, especially in the United States.

There is particular current concern in Britain about redundancy and unemployment, especially when its effects are concentrated dramatically and tragically on a single community like a Welsh mining village, the steel town of Consett or the city of Liverpool. But this is just one of many issues concerning the impact of business on society. Others can be brought to mind readily, simply by mentioning the names of plants or products – Flixborough, Seveso, Three Mile Island, Minnimata, thalidomide, the DC10, asbestos, leaded petrol, cigarettes.

The contemporary relationship between the business enterprise and society forms the broad context within which this book is set. *Private Solutions to Public Problems?* thus refers to the role of free enterprise within contemporary society. In Britain this means that discussion will take place against the background of an evolved *welfare state* in which the virtues of free enterprise are currently being vigorously re-emphasised. The introductory quote is an illustration of this, and deals specifically with the renewal of local economies. Additionally we have recently seen moves to 'privatise' some previously public enterprises, to extend 'choice' in health and education, and to reduce the effect of some *frictional elements* in the labour market.

The role in society of *business*, that is the operations of privately owned firms, or what is often called free enterprise, is a broadly political–ideological issue. Thus business can be seen ideally as providing *private* free-market solutions to the *public* problems of society. In this schema, private entrepreneurs respond freely to market signals and efficiently allocate scarce resources under the spur of competition. Here the economic role of business is associated with the preservation of individual liberty, as in Milton Friedman's linking of capitalism and freedom.

In the United States, nineteenth- and twentieth-century industrialisation took place against the background of an eighteenth-century political theory of liberal democracy. The large modern corporation can, however, be seen as a deviation from the associated ideal of the individual entrepreneur. This is the background against which the concept of *corporate social responsibility* should be seen. It has thus been called an American export product, having received much attention there at various times, most recently in the 1970s. The use of the term social responsibility to label the debate about the social role of the large-scale business enterprise has been termed distinctively American, in that it is a euphemism for a debate which is essentially about capitalism.

Thus, typically in America, the debate is couched in terms of 'business' rather than capitalism. The firm is conventionally regarded as just another organisation, but operating in a social environment in which pressure groups convert political/social demands into constraining market forces through the legislature. In this framework, firms themselves engage in legitimate political activity, for example through lobbying and political contributions.

This pluralist view is the orthodoxy in the United States. In effect there is a *market* for influence, and firms are counselled to manage this market as rationally as they would any other. A recent American management school working paper typifies this approach.[2]

The regulated social/political environment is described as volatile, and firms are advised to adopt a 'regulatory strategy' for each of the stages of the regulation process. At the root of this advice is the idea that the firm has insufficient control over its environment, and that the state is the vital source of such control. The firm may therefore want to influence the state, either encouraging or discouraging the enactment of new regulations, depending on its interests.

If a new regulation has grassroots support, then an opposing firm may attempt to influence the method of regulation and the adequacy of funding for the agency which will enforce it. The functioning of this agency can also be affected by trying to influence features of its design, such as its structure, location and status. This, it is advised, will affect the goals and motives of the key decision-makers and the way they respond to stimuli from the firm. Thus, when the regulations come to be administered, the firm might be able to exploit conflicts of interest between different regulatory agencies, or activate old alliances and professional and personal networks. Together with the use of its own technical know-how, the firm may thus be able to achieve for itself lower standards, cheaper control technology or compliance delays which imply a competitive advantage over less successful firms.

At every stage, the paper points out, the role of the legislators themselves is vital, hence the importance of lobbying and having the right legislators in office, that is those favourable to the interests and ideology of the business community.

The regulation of the firm's social and political environment is thus treated as a process which can be influenced at various stages. The strategic problem is said to be that of locating the key decision-makers, analysing their 'incentive structure', and then matching it with the resources controlled by the firm. Some examples of these resources which are given in the paper are: political campaign donations; the vital technical know-how of the firm which is needed by the regulators; job offers to administrators; the capacity for collective action with other firms; and the formation of coalitions with other groups who may be affected indirectly or who are dependent on the firm.

The paper's author justifies the management of its social/political environment by business by reference to the 'legitimacy crisis' which has arisen. With the growth in the size of the business firm and the parallel departure from the model of a perfectly competitive market, the firm has become 'quasi-public', but at the same time has suffered a loss of public confidence. It must therefore seek a vital resource, namely social legitimacy.

This highlights the fundamental issue, that is the problem of incorporating the big, powerful enterprise within a democratic social/political framework. That this does represent a problem is a view almost universally shared. There are different opinions, of course, on how it should be, and the extent to which it has already been, resolved.

The writing on this theme over the past thirty years by J. K. Galbraith illustrates these points. Writing about American capitalism in 1952, he noted the fading relevance of the free-market model, illustrating the point by referring to the increased concentration of production in the hands of large firms; the existence of barriers to new entrants; the tendency for market prices to be replaced by administered prices; the prevalence of non-price competition; and the increasing management of the economic system by the government. At this time, however, Galbraith also recognised the potential advantages of efficiency and innovation which could result from these developments, and displayed a belief in the effectiveness of 'countervailing powers' in limiting corporate power.

This closely resembles what has remained the orthodox view, but Galbraith's later writings have placed him nearer to those who take a more radical line, emphasising the extent of corporate power and doubts about its linkage to 'public' goals. These have been the twin themes of Galbraith's later works. He spoke of the 'private affluence and public squalor' resulting from the corporation's private obsession with economic growth and its inability to provide 'social' goods in an otherwise affluent society. Later, he characterised the new industrial state as dominated by mature corporations, emancipated from the market and run by a technocratic élite aiming at planning and control. So, by the 1970s, he described a dominating 'planning sector' of the American economy, formed by a thousand giant corporations, which incorporated the state as guarantor of demand, provider of education and research, and lender of last resort, the whole forming what he termed 'the technostructure'.

Against this background, the potentially rarefied concept of corporate social responsibility can be seen in sharper relief, where it can be variously grasped, attacked or dismissed. It is grasped defensively, for example, by those who accept the inevitability of a dynamic relationship between business and society, in which the issue of corporate legitimacy is never settled once and for all, but who would not like to believe that this entailed an inevitable growth either in corporate power or state control. For them, the concept could offer an evolutionary alternative to the polarity implied in the traditional capitalism versus socialism dispute. If this view is firmly held, and not either cynical or self-deluding, then it would lead to the highest significance being attached to corporate social responsibility. It would be seen as 'the result of mutations more akin to the Reformation or Industrial Revolution than to consumerism or the push for racial equality'.[3] At its most grandiose, social responsibility would represent a *paradigm shift* in the relationship between economy and society.

Rather less romantically, others would attack the concept because they regard the corporation as a specialist economic institution which is adequately restrained in, and/or not competent itself to judge, the social interest. Finally, there are those who would dismiss corporate social responsibility as an irrelevant or rhetorical concept when set against the adjudged reality of corporate power and self-interested behaviour.

Although, as we have seen, the corporate social responsibility debate has been especially American, the underlying issues are relevant in Britain and elsewhere. Several reasons have been offered to explain why, despite this relevance, the concept has received so little specific attention here in comparison with the United States.[4] These include the presence of a large element of public ownership; the acceptance and even encouragement by British governments of industrial concentration; the tradition of government intervention in economic and social affairs; the historical pre-eminence of non-business élites in British society, so that less is expected by way of corporate social leadership; and, finally, a management style in Britain which is typically more informal and intuitive, suggests Epstein, than in the United States.

To the extent that these factors, together with the role of trades unions, have inhibited the renewal of a business social responsibility ethos in Britain, some current, mutually reinforcing developments are significant. For example: a reduction in the acceptance, and to some degree the extent of public ownership; the expressed reluctance of the government to intervene in economic and social welfare matters; the introduction of new legislation limiting the political role of trades unions; the encouragement of businessmen, as illustrated in the opening quotation, to adopt a leadership role in society; and, finally, the possible longer-run tendency for the approach to management in Britain to become more Americanised.

These issues form the background to the research upon which this book is based, but it approaches them from a practical rather than grandly theoretical viewpoint. The two-year research project, funded by the Social Science Research Council, focused on individual firms, and more especially their managements. The central questions it posed were as follows. Does corporate responsibility exist in observed managerial practice? In addition to the pursuit of commercial goals, are firms involved in providing private solutions to public problems, perhaps in the fields of redundancy, the quality of working life, equal opportunity or environmental pollution? How do managers perceive the role of their business enterprise in society? Do they feel capable of accepting social responsibilities, or perhaps some rather than others? What appear to be their motivations, both when they are and when they are not involved? What might be the implications of these findings for any effective future extension of the role of business in the provision of private solutions to public problems?

The reasons for this research emphasis on managers, their perceptions and their behaviour, studied in depth within the context of their daily work, are given in the Appendix on 'Theory and Methods of Research'. This choice was based on a review of theories of society and of organisation. The aim was to avoid the tendency of what little empirical work there is on the subject of corporate social responsibility to adopt a theoretically unselfconscious stance. But, apart from being an outcome of this process, the emphasis on managers also reflects the link between the business and society issues and the long-standing debate on the changing nature of the business organisation.

The tendency for the scale of corporations and the concentration of production to grow, for shared ownership to become more widespread and anonymous, and for an associated divorce of ownership from management, have been widely remarked upon. This process, however, now popularly labelled 'the managerial revolution' or 'the managerialist thesis', is associated particularly with Berle and Means' *The Modern Corporation and Private Property*, published fifty years ago. One of their suggestions was that managers would now have some discretion which might result in an effective broadening of corporate objectives. This is because in classical economic theory, the competitive profit-seeking firm was a robot slave of impersonal market forces. But, given a degree of emancipation from the markets for goods and resources, and also from the capital market, firms (guided by their now liberated, post-revolutionary managers) might be expected to display behavioural variations.

8

Our research on corporate social responsibilities therefore centred on managers, their discretion, perceptions and actions as they managed the social *policies* of their firms. Our specific interest was in the reality, or otherwise, of the concept of social responsibility by reference to managerial practice. Also, as this introduction has already shown, the issue has a particular significance in contemporary Britain. In addition, however, we were aware of the background relevance of the research to a lively and long-standing debate about the 'managerial revolution'. Although there is very wide acceptance of the broad 'managerialist thesis', there are still significant uncertainties and differences – essentially about what motivates and constrains managers, about their interests and the extent of their discretion. Within this debate it is quite possible to find writers with opposing values sharing the belief that commitment to the profit motive has not been diluted for the modern manager.

The study of the practical management of corporate social responsibilities will add something to this debate. Equally, the fundamental issues of interpretation within the 'managerialist' debate itself also serve to highlight the problems of understanding such research findings. We have already referred to the possible role of the social responsibility concept and terminology, particularly in the context of the discussion about the nature of American political-economy. How should the concept be interpreted when it appears at the level of corporate organisational behaviour if, for example, the profit motive is still intact either because it is universally valid or because the 'managerial revolution' is more apparent than real?

In such a case, one possibility would be that the concept is useful, either in the classical pursuit of maximum profit or a 'managerialist' variant like 'satisfactory' profit. From a practical management viewpoint, social responsibility might then amount to *managing the business environment*, that is a wide range of social and political issues which might be categorised as 'peripheral' to the main economic mission of the firm, but which are not unimportant to its success.

Could there be a long-run tendency for such issues to come increasingly into the orbit of modern management technique, forming perhaps a *new wave* in a stream of management developments? In a recent review of current thinking on organisational effectiveness by United States consultants McKinsey and Company, it was concluded that the emphasis which has previously been given to organisational structure linked to strategy has gone too far, and that other factors were critically important in accounting for corporate success and should be given more attention. Notably mentioned were management style and especially 'management's guiding concepts'. It was noted that firms designated as 'excellent' explicitly managed a wider range of variables than other companies.

Examples have been suggested of companies with such 'superordinate goals', companies which 'make meaning' – IBM, Proctor and Gamble, and Matsushita – which accept responsibilities to their employees and utilise social and spiritual forces for the organisation's benefit.[5] (In what may be an interesting parallel, a recent account of the modernisation of management in the Soviet Union described the introduction of 'enterprise social plans' as an attempt to uncover 'the social reserves of production'.)[6]

But this *seamless* approach is not typical of firms in Britain today, and certainly not of our case studies, although one of them has a corporate philosophy and style which is similar. Our research thus focuses not on *the* organisation, but on internal processes and conflicts, and on the interactions between managers and elements of the character and circumstances of their firms, out of which will arise their social policies. In studying business–society relations, such research into the day-to-day practice of management is also essential because neither are firms necessarily managed by 'good goldfish'[7] who are totally visible and responsive to the outside world.

2 Managers: Good Goldfish?

We argued in Chapter 1 that the authors who have revised liberal political economy over the past fifty years (for instance Galbraith) have increasingly placed managers in the foreground and charged them with the responsibility of acting as *custodians of a constitutionalised corporation*. Such a view has by no means fully displaced the orthodoxy. Thus, for Friedman, 'good' managers will be single-mindedly dedicated to the pursuit of profit, and in so doing automatically act to the greater happiness of the greatest number. Here, it would be irresponsible for them to act in any other way. Nor can the managerialists convince the Left of the advisedness of de-regulating corporations, and therefore the actions of managers. The extent to which managers may be trusted as spontaneous arbiters of the public interest is also questioned.

In this chapter, we shall look more closely at what is at stake in studying corporate social policies. Regardless of which of the above three positions one prefers, what managers do and the understanding they have of their own actions is a reasonable starting point. The case studies will show how managers understood their own work at four manufacturers, and whether the meaning that work had for them fitted within any particular one of the three positions.

Corporate Social Responsibility

There are two senses in which managers are held 'responsible'. On the one hand, there is the *moral* sense of responsibility, and on the other, there is the *functional* sense. The *moral* sense refers to what is right and wrong, and here, as we have already hinted, the notion of morally responsible action might be quite different, depending on the political economic theory employed. Thus there are different systems of morality. The *functional* sense refers simply to what managers do, their duties, their job descriptions and their *capacity* to solve given problems: their *job responsibilities*. Again, there are different views on what managers' duties actually entail in practice, and on how to interpret management's understanding.

'Social responsibility', in both senses of the term, has had an historical career. On the one hand, definitions of *corporate morality* have changed in radical shifts during the nineteenth and twentieth centuries. What was moral for the New Model Employers[1] of the nineteenth century would by many be seen as morally undesirable today[2] – hence the changing connotations of the term 'paternalism'. On the other hand, the ambit of company *functions* has changed as the state has taken 'responsibility' for unemployment, housing, education and health.

Suggestions abound today that managers should once again assume *moral* and *functional* responsibilities for certain social problems which they have lost to government over the past hundred years or so. In studying managers' current views and practices, we examine whether such a transition is feasible, and if so, what the 'private solution' would imply for management. Before presenting the case studies, we briefly outline some key concepts and theories which claim to understand the nature of modern management.

MANAGERIALISM

The Managerialist Thesis

It is important to consider the *managerialist thesis* because it treats industrial managers as the new social class of the twentieth century. This new class is seen as independent of shareholder control, and can therefore pursue objectives independent from profit-maximisation. On the basis of the separation of ownership and control there comes an 'end to ideology'.[3] This is for two reasons. First, it is argued, technological progress demands an increasingly complex division of labour, and therefore a correspondingly complex and finely graded social structure. The consequences are that originally clear divisions between owners and workers are blurred by the new 'technostructure':[4] distinct capitalist and worker ideologies disappear in the face of progressive technical and social complexity. Secondly, the separation of ownership and control means that the pervasive influence of owners is removed, to be replaced by a 'people's capitalism'[5] with independent and therefore socially responsible managers. These processes are reinforced with the growth of companies which frees managers from market constraints. Increasingly, companies enjoy a controlling share of the market, and the previous market forces which once compelled companies to *maximise* profits have been replaced, it is said, by the pursuit only of 'satisfactory' profits. Indeed, the interests of managers are supposed now to lie in company survival and growth rather than in the size of dividends.

The managerialist thesis strongly implies an increasingly corporate social responsibility on the part of managers. The thesis accords them discretion to arbitrate between a plurality of interests – shareholders, workers, consumers, suppliers, the

14

local community, etc. – resulting in reasonable and socially legitimate compromises. Managers neutrally arbitrate between competing interests rather than simply defend or advance the special interests of their notional employers. Hence the phrase 'good goldfish'.[6] This analogy is used to convey the independence and public visibility of modern managers.

People's Capitalism?

The 'backbone' of the managerialist thesis is the supposition of the separation of ownership and control of corporations.[7] The question of how many companies are 'manager-controlled' – that is, where shareholders are sufficiently dispersed and where managers have sufficient power for owner-control to be minimal – is in doubt. Questions have been raised over the threshold of dispersal above which a company could reasonably be said to be owner-controlled. Managerialists tend to give a low threshold, which would mean that the majority of corporations are 'manager-controlled'. Others, however, have suggested first, that this level is too low and in any case arbitrary, and secondly, that as long as there is one moderately large shareholder amongst many small ones, then power can easily be exercised. Further, there is no *guarantee* that 'dispersed' shareholders will not exercise their collective control over managers.

Even if it could be agreed that any given company was manager-controlled, there remains the question of whether managers would exercise their discretion in opposition to normal business objectives. As we shall see below, it is feasible to argue that manager-controlled companies are *more* likely to be dedicated solely to the pursuit of profit. Here, we have different conceptions as to what managers are. Managerialists

15

posit a class made up of many *individuals*, and distinct as a group only in so far as they are each independent of owners and workers. In contrast, others such as Erik Olin Wright[8] see the managerial class in terms of an ambiguous collectivity torn between the two great camps. The higher a manager's position, the more likely he will be a prisoner of a capitalist imperative, whilst middle and junior managers may be subjected to more divided loyalties towards conflicting shareholder and worker interests. Clearly, this view, with its emphasis on the persistence of class ideology, and with its assertion of a dualistic model of society, takes us well away from the good goldfish analogy.

Our case studies explore these contrasting conceptions of managers by stating managers' views of their own work.

Bureaucracy and Career

The managerialists state that the modern industrial bureaucracies are so large and powerful in themselves that shareholder interests can no longer dominate. On a day-to-day basis it is managers who manage. Despite this, within bureaucracies, however large, it is nevertheless assumed that managers are more than mere cogs in a machine, and have the discretion to arbitrate between competing interests. (Critics might detect a contradiction in these two statements.) Bureaucracies are supposed to offer a 'responsible autonomy' to managers, which allows them to be good goldfish. The opposite position is that bureaucracies are *capitalist* bureaucracies in essence, emerging as more perfected institutions for the pursuit of profits. Under this schema management remains weak in itself, being controlled by shareholder interests, and controlling subordinates on their behalf. Thus, for the managerialist thesis, power starts with managers – shareholders are but one amongst many constituents. For the Left, as well as orthodox political-economists, power starts with shareholder interests, the capitalist organisation disciplining managers accordingly.

Managers not only have organisations for which to work, but also have careers to make. Given that the managerialists and the radicals (conservative and Marxist) have different views of where power lies, it is not surprising that they take very different views on the question of career. The underlying assumption of the managerialist thesis here is that individual managers, like all members of society, draw their power and influence from the consensus. The more managers are in harmony with the majority views of a pluralist society, the more likely they are to have a successful career. The central purpose of the organisation, therefore, is to make sure that managers' actions conform to the consensus. Organisations which succeeded in producing responsive managers would, under this model, correspondingly gain legitimacy in the public eye. In this way, corporations are, in the last instance, also controlled by the consensus.

It is, however, possible to start from the question of bureaucracy career and control and come up with rather different conclusions. If one sees businesses as irredeemably connected with shareholder interests that are in conflict with other (especially working-class) interests, then the discipline exerted on managers by their bureaucracy merely ties them more effectively to shareholders' interests. Of course, for consensus managerialism this is no problem, as shareholder interests (among others) are legitimate, and therefore their pursuit by managers is socially authoritative. In addition, there is no automatic assumption for consensus managerialists that shareholder interests are necessarily in essential contradiction to other interests.

Radicals take exactly the opposite view. Bureaucracies and career structures serve to bind the manager to shareholder interest more than to any supposed consensus. They would be cynical of any 'responsible autonomy' granted to managers by their bureaucracies. Rather, careers might be seen as the insidious means whereby managers are more completely incorporated into the instrumental objectives of the corporation as a whole, and ultimately its owners. So long as managers' performances are measured using the criteria of profit-maximisation, they will *actively* seek to underline shareholder interests. Social responsibility to other constituents would necessarily have a lower value from this perspective, because other interests are seen as being in contradiction to shareholder interests. Alan Berkeley Thomas has thus argued that the relatively high levels of discretion enjoyed by managers in modern corporations are afforded not because managers are beyond the control of shareholder interests, but because allowing discretion secures managerial commitment and compliance to shareholder interests.[9]

The existence of these competing views of bureaucracy and career should make us particularly sensitive to the comments managers make about their understanding of their own careers.

Finally, there are some sociologists who would argue that because managers have only limited discretion, then the very act of studying them may distract attention from 'master institutions' in society. For instance, Gouldner[10] suggests that the very act of studying managers implies that managers are somehow responsible for social problems, whereas they may be no more than 'flak catchers' and 'middle dogs' who are compelled to work within fundamental constraints. To study managers in relation to 'social responsibility' would have been especially objectionable to him, in that the notion could be interpreted as implicitly holding managers both accountable and responsible for public problems. Accepting this criticism, there is still a justification in studying managers, for the *limits* of managerial discretion and corporate social policies will be apparent. Moreover, as our case studies show, detailed attention to what managers do reveals the way in which broader political processes become resolved. Regardless of the position one takes, managerialist, conservative or radical, there is much at stake and there are beliefs to test in studying managers.

BUSINESS WELFARISM

The contrasting managerial cultures and ideologies which we shall come across in the case studies reveal something of the changing career which the concept of 'corporate social responsibility' has itself gone through in Britain and America.

The British Case

In Britain, the mid-nineteenth century saw a comprehensive transition in political and economic theory and practice, during which social problems were for the first time seen to be a collective responsibility. Initially, those owner-managers who could best afford to, offered healthier and safer working conditions, provided company houses, developed the paternalistic manifesto of 'civic gospel' and of the 'New Model Employers',[11] and generally initiated what was to become known as the 'voluntary tradition' in local welfare service provision. As we noted above, it soon became clear to this group of progressive and advanced industrialists that there were competitive economic limits upon the private solutions they could provide individually. The public political declarations of these manufacturers made it clear that state intervention was entirely legitimate. The state was seen as more

19

economically efficient, in that if collective state services were provided and the costs borne equally among all businesses, then the competitive disadvantages of providing direct solutions by themselves could be obviated. At the same time, the general health, education and social stability of the population at large would be increased to the employers' perceived benefit.

In Britain, there was something of a convergence between civic gospel and socialist manifestos – 'municipal socialism' – to produce the political will to build what would become a welfare state.[12] The very development of these services and the acceptance by the state of 'social responsibilities' directly undermined the voluntary tradition of business welfarism. This was not altogether a smooth process, but it did provide for an accommodation between business interests and the labour movement which is very substantially intact today.

Chamberlain, Birmingham's famous social reformer of the 1870s, and himself a manufacturer, campaigned successfully for municipalisation in direct variance to earlier *laissez-faire* political-economy. A private company, he argued, was *necessarily* bound to private interests. The pursuit of private interests was legitimate, he believed, but only to a definite point. There was a necessity for collective provision, for 'the power of life and death should not be left in the hands of a commercial company but should be conducted by the representatives of the people'. Avery, Chamberlain's political ally and fellow businessman, elaborated that it was 'the duty of a wise local government to endeavour to surround the humbler classes of the population with its benevolent and protecting care'. Similarly, in Bristol, the Frys and Wills, chocolate and tobacco manufacturers, 'were moved to urge on the council a more positive role on behalf of all citizens'.[13]

The emergence of civic gospel, among usually nonconformist, owner-managers, was a widespread phenomenon. Equally important to note is that the very industrialists that Mr

Heseltine apparently had in mind (see page 1) were often *positively hostile* towards private solutions to public problems.

Once absolved of their 'responsibilities' which they were willing to see developed by the state, industrialists could then get on with the business of increasing their own companies' fortunes or with their leisure pursuits. Considerable increases in working-class welfare both at work and outside were enshrined in the emergent welfare state.

This development is, as we shall show, very much stamped on the practice of two of our companies, Davis's and Parker's, who 'treat the outside world like the weather', and are happy to have seen a socialisation of social and communal responsibilities. As one director says, 'It's a national government problem, not ours.' Both these cases reflect the evolution of a political accommodation particular to social democracy in the western European sense. Freed from sentimental obligation and paternal 'responsibilities', managers at Davis's, for instance, could now safely concentrate their efforts on economic performance, and worry themselves far less with civic involvement than did their owner-managing predecessors. Here, indeed, the geographical spreading out of ownership made the shareholders far less interested, in any case, in the character of the particular community in which Davis's operates.

The American Case

However, one case study differs drastically from this position, being American owned and controlled and reflecting the American political tradition. The flavour of American corporate thinking is different from that of British companies who, as we shall see in the third case study especially, are at home with the welfare state. In America, corporations are far more prepared to involve themselves in community affairs and

politics. Whilst there *has* been a divestment of social responsibilities to the American welfare state, corporations have been,
and continue to be, far more reluctant collectivists than are
their British counterparts. The continuing domestic political
activism of American corporations thus contrasts with the
relative political quiescence of British companies. Many
American companies take political action to keep the state at
bay. American managers are, therefore, more accustomed to
political activism defensive of the private realm. They defend
the legitimacy of the corporation in terms of a promise of
private solutions to public problems. This contrast poses the
question of what American companies will do *in Britain*.

In our fourth case study we shall see how the American way
has been built into Pedigree Petfoods management. Against the
British historical trend, Petfoods is increasingly moving towards the American norm, thus possibly forming a New Wave
here. It has even mooted the idea of forming a 'one per cent
club'. Very common in the United States,[14] such clubs of
successful businesses contribute to various community projects
from private corporate sources.

Although we do not wish to overdraw this comparison (for
when one stands back from the rhetoric, British and American
businesses have much in common), it is nevertheless generally
true that the politics of the corporation and the incorporation of
worker interests have taken somewhat different paths in the
two countries. Certainly, American business was more fearful
of the formation of socialist parties than was British business.
The tacit accommodation between 'civic gospel' and municipal
socialism in Britain consequently lacks an American counter-
part. Thus, where the New Deal acted as a stimulant to a
politically defensive managerialism in America, the welfare
state *fulfilled* the manifesto of progressive industrialists, and
therefore acted to depress the political activity of business in
Britain.

POLICY AND THEORY

Two Managerialisms

Assuming that the comparisons we have sketched out are reasonable approximations of the comparative development of the United States and United Kingdom, one can go on to identify corresponding differences of managerial doctrine.

In America the managerialist thesis is generally associated with an explicit political doctrine and morality. In Britain, however, managerialism does not appear to have received the weight of attention that American academics have given it, all the managerialist 'classics' having been written from America. If there is a British doctrine of managerialism, then it would seem to be implicit rather than explicit and, on the evidence of most of the managers on whom we shall report (below), appears to be apolitical. Again, British management doctrine seems to adopt a different social morality to that of the American architects of managerialism – Berle and Means, Chester Barnard, James Burnham.

Setting out the American doctrine first, it of course proceeds beyond the core assumptions – separation of control from ownership, the neutrality of the state, the development of monopoly – to the first substantive proposition that managers are now in a position to arbitrate between competing interests. Because corporations are in the hands of the ideologically neutral, a socially credible mechanism for resolving conflicts has been created. So it is argued. More than this, the undeniable impression given by most managerialist writing is of a defensive capitalism that would have managerially-controlled firms directly providing private solutions to public problems. It is this drift that informs the greater part of the 'corporate social responsibility debate'. While not necessarily (in theory) against public solutions, most managerialists, especially as they are addressing themselves to an American gallery, seem to be trying to keep the state at bay.

In short, the good goldfish are good both because of their supposed independence and because they can deliver the solution. It is on the basis of the consequent 'self-socialisation' of major corporations ('corporate socialism', 'social responsibility', the 'mature corporation') and on the basis of a 'new code of ethics' that Berle and his supporters assert the legitimacy of the corporation in principle.[15] This is clearly a political statement, as it seeks to alter the political agenda in favour of the corporation – albeit neutral and 'responsive'.

British managerial doctrine is not charged with this mission. Indeed, because state intervention appears to have been accepted or even promoted in the past by business, managers today are, in an important sense, apolitical. Because they have not seen it as so necessary to defend the private against the public realm, managerialism as such has not been developed in Britain. It is, therefore, necessary to ask managers what they think of their responsibilities (moral and functional) in order to find out what British managerialism is. While the library shelves contain many essays in (American) managerialism, British managerialism is an unwritten subject.

The evidence from our case studies will show that, contrary to American managerialism, British *managers* believe that state responsibility in the economy, and especially for social welfare, is desirable. We find little of the American managerialists' promotion of the private realm to exclude the public realm. Indeed, the lack of interest shown by British managers in setting political agendas seems to indicate that they, rather than American managers, are the ones who are politically neutral. In our first three case studies, managers minded only what they saw as their own businesses, and left public problems for others to look after. Said one: 'We pay government to look after unemployment . . . it's a government responsibility, not ours.' British managerialism – that is, the doctrines of British managers at work – does not promise private solutions. American managerialism, in principle, does.

Given these differences, it is particularly important to contrast the first three of our cases, where managers are content to be relieved of social responsibility by the state, with Pedigree Petfoods, where managers incorporate social responsibility as a necessary part of the defence and extension of their company's market and legitimacy.

This contrast and the contrasting biographies of managers at the companies – biographies which largely explain the managerial doctrines chosen – provide the essence of this book. We shall suggest that the question of how, why and where management beliefs are generated is of great importance in determining how readily the responsibility for public problems might be privatised in Britain.

A Dilemma for British Managers

Calls for businesses to reinvolve themselves 'in the community' present managers, especially British managers, with a dilemma. We have argued that managers in Britain have become increasingly apolitical in the sense of being relieved of a mass of 'social responsibilities' by the welfare state. They are quite prepared to see government 'own the problem' and enjoy perceived advantages in having the state provide education, housing, health care, and unemployment cover, as well as infrastructures such as roads and railways. This means that they can get on with 'minding their own businesses'.

On the other hand, boardroom banter generally has it that the state is an inefficient provider, is costly and over-developed, and ought to 'get off the backs of wealth creators'. Thus

25

managers on the one hand enjoy the services furnished by the state and the relief of much responsibility that this brings, and on the other, have an object of derision.

This long-standing post-War ambivalence towards the public realm may be tested in the near future. If the current call for 'private solutions' is essentially a political rallying cry and little more, and the state will continue to 'own' the problem, then British managers will remain very much as they have been for the last forty years or so, their ambivalence untested. If, however, the request is taken seriously by government, then managers will indeed be asked to devise the beginnings of a local community role. Managers may ask what it is that the government expects of them. Do they have to 'go round the stump of local politics' – as did so many progressive nineteenth-century industrialists? Are they expected to bear social responsibility (functional and moral) for community problems like unemployment? Are they expected to provide *successful* or only partial solutions? And are they expected to form a new, active élite?

The case studies will show how the American managerialism and British management doctrine would react so differently to a request for 'private solutions' and, through an examination of managers' biographies, provide some observations on which an estimate of the nature of the outcome might be made.

The reader's reaction to our evidence will partly turn on his or her own stance. For many of the New Wave to whom the notion of private solutions strongly appeals, the prospect of the politically reactivated corporation and of the politically involved manager will be welcomed. The European Societal Strategy Project's *Facing Realities*[16] argues directly that businessmen

will need to understand, appreciate and act upon the changes which have taken place. Most importantly, they

26

must assume responsibility not only for running the business but also for shaping the economic, social and political environment in which their firms operate.

For others, the prospect of managers reinvolving themselves in community affairs may be a more disturbing one. For them, it would be much better that they keep their hands off public problems.

Whichever way one chooses, the question of whether corporations should take a consciously active part (formal and informal) in Britain's social life appears to be back on the agenda. Our case studies should provide a basis for discussion here and in the future. The way the situation will develop will partly depend on the comparative evolution of British and American political cultures.

Managerial ideology is a necessary part of national political arrangements. One eye should, therefore, be kept on any changes at the national level in Britain that may herald the political reawakening of British managers and a shift towards the American pattern. The other eye should be directed at managers for signs of any response to the government's reassertion of the virtues of the private over the public realm. Any corresponding evolution in British business school thinking towards a new political philosophy for managers should also be watched for. But, above all, the biographical experience of British managers, the generational differences between a New School and an Old School, and the organisational anthropology of individual British and American corporations must provide the best point of focus for a grounded theory. Against the background of theoretical and historical debate we therefore feature the kinds of managers involved: their generational differences, biographies, ideologies and organisational cultures.

Any exploration of social questions by way of case study

necessarily involves telling a story in which many elements are balanced. However, we shall try to make clear which features we see as the most important. It is for others to judge whether we 'tell it as it is'.

3 'The Successful Integration of Foreign Labour'

We were invited by Harveys Foundry to study its 'successful integration of foreign labour'. Harveys believes that there is 'no problem round here'. This chapter is concerned to explain how it is that managers and the trades unions believe that black labour has been 'successfully integrated'. They defined this largely in terms of the absence of public intervention, and thus our account concentrates on internal organisational features of the company.

William Harvey established the Phoenix Iron Works in a West Midlands town in the last century. At its zenith, Harveys was amongst the most advanced foundries in Europe, both technically and managerially, although it has since lost its leading position. It is still engaged in the manufacture of general engineering castings, although it is attempting to develop capacity in the production of specialist castings for new markets. While employment peaked in the mid-1950s at more than 2000 workers, today the company employs less than 1000. Numbers gradually declined to about 1500 up to 1970, although production rose by 25 per cent during this period, indicating increasing labour productivity through mechanisation. Numbers were steady until recently when, over a two-year period, the labour force was reduced to less than 1000. New mechanised moulding plants and core shops were introduced

29

to the plant in the late 1950s and 1960s, and various other innovations, including annealing ovens, have also been introduced since the 1950s. The recent rounds of redundancies have not, however, been technically induced. While the most advanced foundries in Britain have begun to automate their plants, Harveys has experienced a drastic decline in output.

At the end of the Second World War Harveys was a labour-intensive company. An ex-works-director explained that 'had we invested during the war in mechanical production then we wouldn't have had to recruit labour. Outfits like Harveys were labour intensive', with, for example, metal moved manually from furnaces to casting teams in 'bogies' of about half a ton. Even before the war, 'foreign labour' had been employed. Harveys took on refugees from the Spanish Civil War as well as a succession of European nationalities including Poles and Irishmen. In some cases, William Harvey, the then chairman, had paid their passages. Post-war, foreign labour became increasingly necessary because of the backward technical nature of the plant, heavy industry being less attractive to whites. White workers also shunned Harveys because the practice had been to take on and lay off labour according to demand with the seasons. This annual lay-off of up to 150 men as demand fell became increasingly unacceptable to whites, with the tight labour market of the 1950s. So long as the practice continued, it was increasingly difficult to attract whites. The ex-works-director said 'the traditional type of British workman' could no longer be attracted. There had been, he added, a political evolution in the working class, and this practice in the labour market had been rejected. 'So it meant filling up with coloured labour.' Indeed, as in other Midlands towns, a 'dual labour market' has developed, with white factories and black factories. Harveys is a black factory, with about 70 per cent categorised as 'foreign'.[1]

Ownership and Control

Harveys became a public company between the wars. However, the family remained in control of the board and continued to be the company's largest shareholders. So strong had been the control by the family, that many of its managers did not realise that it had been a public company for so long. The personnel manager, for instance, told us that the company went public only six years ago. Eventually, however, its bankers became increasingly influential. With a growing financial crisis, they insisted on rationalisation, including workforce redundancies, and are reputed to have had some influence on boardroom appointments. Thus, whilst the Harvey dynasty passed down the chairmanship and managing directorship for decades, and while the whole board traditionally was made up of 'family and friends', this pattern has by now been broken down. A number of accounts suggested that there had always been conflicts within the board as to the direction the company might take. However, the subsequent boardroom changes probably represented a significant development in the company's politics. The present incumbents are mobile and ambitious, with fewer effective ties to the company.

Despite the changes at the top, the old patterns of status, authority and organisation remain largely intact, down to the level of 'junior management' (a grade which includes the personnel manager!). Status divisions are still symbolised in the location of offices and their decor – the family occupied the inner sanctum in a grandly embellished Edwardian building; other directors and senior managers the top floor of a newer administrative block; and middle and junior managers the lower floors. We found the three personnel staff (including the manager) and their secretary in a small, old, poorly lit building. The canteen is partitioned according to status, although the food is the same, and directors have their own dining room.

Workers were obviously aware of these implied differences: workers and foremen we interviewed in the old Edwardian building were bemused at ever having been allowed in.

The directors of Harveys Foundry are 'split down the middle'. On the one hand are the foundrymen and on the other there are the managers. Foundrymen are imbued in an industrial culture – they 'know what castings are all about' – while managers describe themselves as pure organisers. One senior manager said: 'I'm basically a manufacturing man, but I'm not a foundryman. I don't think you have to be. It's a tradition to be a foundryman. I'm not one. I'm a manager.'

Below board level the foundrymen predominate. They have typically devoted their entire working lives to Harveys, often following in the footsteps of their kin, and are thus slow to be replaced. In the early 1960s, a new pattern of recruitment based on professional qualification rather than practical knowledge and seniority was instigated. So far, however, the lack of openings due to the incumbency of foundrymen has meant that it has had little impact. Redundancies throughout the 1970s and early 1980s, being based on the traditional rule of 'last in, first out', have reinforced this situation.

Foundrymen know the works 'like the backs of their hands', know 'how and when to give a bollocking', know that their authority is not diminished if occasionally they 'shout the roof off', because they are also known to be committed to 'their men'. They have demonstrated this commitment by showing that they are prepared 'to get their hands dirty if necessary'. Generally, they feel they are on the retreat and believe the old days were best. They describe the self-styled professional managers as no more than 'whizz-kids', and blame them for the crisis the company currently faces.

Professional managers, a minority below board level, see themselves as the 'new blood' in which the future of Harveys is invested. One complained of the *ad hoc* character of foundrymen management: 'We tend here not to plan properly for the future. I think we should.' The managers do not necessarily have foundry qualifications, and do not see themselves as dependent on the company, or even the foundry industry, for their careers. They believe in 'making your own luck'. They are young and more geographically mobile than foundrymen, and thus find shopfloor culture alien. In their estimation it is the foundrymen's lack of innovative ability – both technical and organisational – that is largely at the root of Harveys' crisis.

'SUCCESSFUL INTEGRATION'

Harveys managers report that 'foreign labour' has been 'successfully integrated', and in an important sense this view is justified. During the case study many overtly racist comments from foremen and white shop stewards were recorded; equally, however, in practice shopfloor race relations were mostly at least amicable and often comradely and mutually respectful. On the one hand, foremen made racist, though typically contradictory, statements:

> Basically the coloureds don't work as well as a white man. They plot, using the Race Relations Act. You get a bit more out of a West Indian, but you don't get value for money from Asians unless you stand over them.
> I mix and listen with the National Front, but I like the coloured way of life because their wives live, and are brought up, not to make the men's lives a misery. They've got a lot of respect for men. Men dread having daughters and want to get them off their hands. It's his mother, then his sister who come before his wife. There is less violence towards parents

as there is in the Western way of living . . . [But] look at the way they're kicking the police to death.

Coloured labour on my part is a very sore point. They're using it against us. When they're bargaining with you they won't let you get a word in. Try to understand them? You just can't.

White shop stewards also expressed some racist comments along similar lines.

On the other hand, shopfloor relations, as we noted, were in practice far more amicable than these comments from some foremen and shop stewards might imply. Most foremen had come to recognise that cultural differences existed which could 'come across' as offensive in the absence of that knowledge. For example:

from a working point of view, these people's broken English can sound very demanding. You've got to be understanding of their linguistics. They sound aggressive and demanding when really they're trying to say 'please give me some overtime'. Actually they say 'Give me overtime!'

Some foremen were even aware of differences *within* cultures. For instance, while some Indians are 'aggressive' in their speech, others are 'too polite':

Most Indians take a long time coming to the point. One day one brought me a cup of tea. The next day he came and asked me for some more overtime! Having said that, Harveys would be in a mess without them . . . I get on with them all right.

While some foremen were unable to come fully to terms with cultural differences in communication, a majority had, either through practice or conscious effort. One emphasised how foremen have to 'reassure' Asians that their swearing is not meant as an offence. Just as foremen have had to come to terms with Asian culture, so too do Asians have to be taught the ways of British shopfloor culture. They have to learn, for instance, that being called a 'bastard' is not necessarily abusive, and is more often a term of affection reserved only for accepted friends(!).

Likewise, the white shop stewards, while reserving some racist comments, have found black labour easily unionised and reliable allies in industrial bargaining. Thus, although initially stating that race relations were 'very poor' and that Asians were 'a treacherous race', a senior white shop steward added that he got on very well with the Indian shop steward in the fettling shop: 'I get on with him very well – he has integrated. The Indians are very good union people. You have no problem getting them to join the union.' Another said: 'They believe in the unions completely. It's a must with them.' The election of the first black shop steward has been 'an enormous shock' to the then convenor, another shop steward reported. However, since then another four black workers have been shop stewards, and they have won the respect of other trades unionists by gaining a reputation for very hard bargaining. Indeed, one ex-shop-steward, now foreman, told us that he had ousted a shop steward who was 'a terrible racist'. According to him, 'you couldn't have trouble because people depend on one another. I have to contain it. People work here in a team, they come in together.'

Acceptance of black labour by the trades unions can, of course, compromise relations between black labour and fore-men, especially given this reputation for 'abrasive' bargaining. The convenor told us that in one case there was 'a bit of a problem' because a black shop steward 'didn't get on with his foreman'. There was 'a certain amount of resentment'. The foreman himself explained the situation:

To be a shop steward you've got to learn to talk to the person (the foreman), to give both ways, you know, and this one, he doesn't ask, he comes and *demands* – he wants, he wants, and he wants. . . . The convenor has been here more times in the last three months than in the whole of my time here.

What the black shop steward reported to us as being his duty, the foreman saw as a break with the past. The steward said that his predecessor had been too much in the pockets of the foreman. From the foreman's point of view, the election of a black steward had 'been a source of trouble. The shop was running fairly well before he became a shop steward; at one period if a cleaning machine broke down, work was passed on to trimming "dirty", and he stopped this.' The steward had also established certain demarcations, stopped unlicensed forklift truck driving, and is currently trying to change piecework prices.

Thus, although some racist comments were recorded from white shop stewards, as in the case of the foremen's comments above, the reality of race relations was far more favourable than this would suggest. White stewards emphasised that the differences between black and white workers had become far less important than the differences that separated workers collectively from management.

Through joking relations, both the remaining tensions *and* the solidarity of the whole workforce are resolved. For example, one superintendent said: 'The foreman used to scream, "Rasta, you black bastard . . ." but it was friendly banter. They used to make tea together.' He went on to say that he had just come back from a holiday on the Mediterranean; he made jokes to the Indian workers, by rolling up his sleeve and comparing skin colour. 'Look, I've wasted two hundred pounds to get the same colour as you. They take it as a joke. It doesn't mean anything.'

To insiders, these jokes are readily understood, and in fact all workers are skilful in differentiating between apparent and real insults. For instance, one superintendent had initially been worried that a 'racial thing' was being started when a Jamaican complained of being called a 'thieving black bastard'. He made an official complaint, but to the relief of the superintendent it later became clear that it was not being called a 'black bastard' to which he took offence, but the word 'thieving'!

There was, then, a lack of overt racial conflict, and most foremen could recall no more than one or two instances in their long careers at Harveys. The most often cited case was of the company's objection to a high status Indian's display of his ceremonial knife. But even here the issue did not come to a head, because this employee chose to leave the company, it is said for other reasons.

To summarise, it is by such evidence of a lack of tension, and indeed of a real camaraderie on the shopfloor,[2] that management can refer to a 'successful integration of foreign labour', and could indeed be confident that our case study would 'find no problem round here'.

INEQUALITIES

The 'successful integration' (shopfloor camaraderie) which we have documented above cannot be underestimated in importance, and is a vital first step towards full racial equality. However, there is equally important evidence of unconscious discrimination. This turns on certain assumptions at senior and middle management levels. To understand these, we must refer to the historical processes by which discrimination has been institutionalised.

As we noted above, 'foreign labour' was recruited in the first place for its cheapness and willingness to comply with unpleasant working conditions and heavy discipline.[3] We also saw that black labour had been retained after the implementation of mechanisation; however, some of the derogatory assumptions initially made about 'foreign labour' by management have been sustained, despite improved working conditions and gradual elimination of differences between blacks and whites on the shopfloor. Before detailing institutionalised discrimination, we shall first mention the advances which have been made by black workers.

In the early days of immigrant labour, blacks were concentrated in the worst jobs in the foundry – the 'donkey jobs'. Additionally, the gang system[4] was predominant; although some blacks were accepted into these exclusive groups, in many cases management was forced to maintain all-black and all-white gangs to work separately. By successive stages – which were often marked by conflicts establishing new custom and practice – blacks have today gained access to all departments except maintenance. One major instance concerned the proposal to employ blacks on 'machine jobs' in a new moulding line opened in the late 1960s. This is remembered by some old foremen as the major turning point. One recalled that two black workers were sent down by management to work on the line, but at that time 'moulding was a class distinction job – they weren't allowed to work the machines'. Said one manager, 'the unions were very very firm on this. . . . Yes, it was very difficult in those days.' The shop stewards were called in by the moulders, and the foremen called in senior management. They argued continuously for three hours. The matter was eventually solved in two ways: by citing the then new Race Relations Act, and by management agreeing that black workers would first have to prove on probation that they were capable. Previously:

only the English and the Irish were allowed to work the moulding machines: no coloureds. We had the first two coloured workers down here for four or five hours on the line, before the shop stewards could be convinced to let them work.

Here, management were obliged to attack shopfloor and union racism in order to meet manning requirements. Similar instances in the 1960s marked the access of blacks to successive shops, and these acts on the part of management clearly contributed to the formation of the shopfloor camaraderie we have detailed. However, this is as far as management 'commitment' to racial equality has so far developed, and in the case of promotions to foremen, management has altered traditional requirements. One of the effects is to make it virtually impossible for blacks to become foremen. The absence of black foremen is indeed striking, especially in those shops where black labour constitutes up to 80 or 90 per cent of the workforce.

With the implementation of new technology in the 1950s and 1960s, the works director instituted the *technically-trained foreman* to replace the man who had 'come up from the shopfloor'. There was now, he said, a shortage of 'very high calibre British workers [although] there are still some of them left'. Promotion on seniority, which would have ultimately favoured black labour, was replaced by a system based on educational certificates. Thus a recruitment division was established in a double sense between management and the shopfloor, barring at once blacks and the non-technically educated. The result is that although some shops have approaching 90 per cent black labour, there are no black foremen or chargehands at Harveys. The new recruitment system was necessary, it was explained by the works director, 'simply because there was no longer the intake of the calibre of chap we had had in the past'. This divide was the price paid not simply for introducing mechanised plants in the 1950s and 1960s – the official reason – but also for preventing the access of blacks, originally recruited for *heavy manual processes*, to even the lower management grades.

Both the new and old schools of lower managers have repeatedly drawn our attention to this transition and its implications. As one old foreman put it,

> the days of the 'foreman' as such are practically finished. If Harveys survives it will be 'superintendents'; they'll all have gone to college. Now you've got more superintendents than foremen; they're all over the place. It was the retired works director who introduced the 'young blood' as he used to call it.

Of course, those blacks who might otherwise have expected to take up foremanship on grounds of seniority are faced now by an evident change of rationale which excludes them from consideration. In so far as they accept the legitimacy of technical training, they cannot attack what, in the opinion of some of them, is a form of discrimination.

When foremen and shop stewards were asked whether they could envisage black foremen or superintendents at Harveys in the future, and whether there was a senior management policy on black labour, the *institutional* character of the problem became clear. To the first question, some answered 'yes' and some 'no'. Those answering 'yes' reflected the general recognition on Harveys' shopfloor that 'barring the smell of curry they're the same as us'. In other words, they no longer recognised *racial* qualities which might debar blacks from foremanship in principle. Those answering 'no' often agreed with this non-racist assessment, but were pointing out that because of the introduction of college educational requirements, the chances of a black from *Harveys' own workforce* becoming a foreman or superintendent were nil. The crucial point here is that neither response was racist, and yet the institution of 'technical' promotion continued to have the effect of discriminating by race. Thus the original opinion held of blacks by certain senior managers when 'foreign labour' was first set on has today become fossilised. The old view was evidenced in the works director's comments about the lack of 'high calibre' workers. These views were central to the then new criteria for promotion – the new blood – and continue to be incorporated, albeit unwittingly, and even in contradiction to the increasing recognition of parity of racial ability on the shopfloor.

To the second question, as to whether there was a senior management policy on black labour, everybody said no. Today nobody sees the technical criteria for promotion as a senior management policy *on black labour*. Its legitimacy is based on its almost unanimous current perception as a straightforward policy *on new promotion criteria for new technology*, whatever might have been the mix of original motives. But there are a number of doubts cast on its validity. For example, old foremen are often found today in the most advanced sections of the factory, while some 'new bloods' are found in the least advanced. In these cases, possession of technical training thus seems to be relatively unimportant. Also, the college-trained superintendents are themselves often dismissive of any advantages that they learned from the old foremen than from Foundry College. As one said, 'our hands are as dirty as theirs'. Finally, there would be a conceivable advantage in having black foremen supervising black shops, in terms of language and communications.

'NO GRIPES'

Most black workers at Harveys generally accept their situation. Some tacitly accept the technical rationale, while others are suspicious. They found themselves having to admit that black people 'can't say they're qualified enough'. One added that while this situation would be tolerated for the present, young generation blacks are likely to fight for an equal chance – 'they won't stand for it'. He suggested that, in the meantime, 'it's not our fight', finding prejudice currently 'very subtle and hard to explain'.

Part of this subtlety is that the 'point of discrimination' is outside the factory gates – in this case, technical foundry apprentices, the future superintendents, are recruited from local schools, and therefore out of a population which does not contain the concentration of blacks which are found in the works. The result is, and will continue to be, that in any batch of college graduates, the numbers of blacks will be small. So far, no blacks have been recruited via this means.

Although considerable advances have been made within the union, removing a legacy of overt racism, there is still a tendency not to have black issues on the agenda. This is for two reasons. Firstly, only one of the five blacks with experience as shop stewards has seen his role as consciously to represent black interests, and even here this was limited to the question of unpaid leave. More characteristically, black shop stewards cited familiar trades union aspirations as their motives for standing for election. Secondly, the union, even in the case of unpaid leave, has preferred to put central wage-bargaining issues on the table. One black shop steward reported that the union had said: 'Let's cool it – let's get wages out of the road, then we'll go for unpaid leave.' He was still waiting to hear something at the time of the research. There is a lack of consciousness of black issues on the part of the union.

The small supply of black nominees for shop steward elections is probably related to the legacy of racial tension that pre-dated 'successful integration' on the shopfloor. Like managers, the union is no longer racist, yet still the new agenda has not been developed. Probably more important for the delay in forming the new agenda, however, is the fact that with Harveys' economic decline over the last few years, there have been heavy redundancies, including the foreman grades; that is, there have been few opportunities for promotion in any case.

MANAGEMENT POLICY

Under these circumstances it becomes understandable how senior management can get by without a policy on black labour. Thus one summarised: 'You only need a policy if you've got a problem. . . . I don't think we have.' Indeed at all levels including senior management, it suffices that new workers are set on by the personnel department, regardless of their colour, and that there are today 'coloureds in all departments'.[5] A director said: 'There's no senior management policy because, to be honest, to be frank, I don't think there's been a call for one. . . . I don't think anything at all was ever done. I shrugged my arms and said, "What the hell?".'

Except for one or two critical incidents such as the abolition of 'class distinction jobs', senior management have delegated 'successful integration' to the foremen. Said a senior foreman:

They don't say anything about coloured integration. That's entirely left to the foreman. Where the foreman puts his lad, whether he's coloured or white, that's entirely up to the foreman. It's entirely up to the foreman to know his team. You have to treat each person individually.

Management policy, union policy, and shopfloor black perceptions, are tied up with each other. For black labour, there is an awareness of the 'subtlety' of the race problem and the unlikelihood of promotions in the near future. For the union, issues concerned with black labour are, largely for these reasons, not an issue because it has been 'successfully integrated' and poses no problems. These circumstances simply do not hold for any of the corresponding parties at our second case-study firm.

4 Treating the Outside World like the Weather

Parker Foods is a food manufacturer with plants on several sites in a south-west Midlands city which chronicle the firm's successes to date. Parker's *is* a successful company. Parker's employs something under 2000 people, and its current share of the market is above 20 per cent and rising quickly. Indeed, the plant just opened is gearing up to take advantage of a demand for their products that was not envisaged even seven years ago. Today, Parker's employs the most modern food-processing technology.

Set up after the war by the Parker family as a very small local concern, the firm expanded rapidly from the late 1960s onwards. Soon afterwards, the family felt financially over-extended with the rapid expansion of an under-capitalised business, and they sold out to American Foods of the United States. It was hoped that the Americans would preserve local managerial autonomy, and therefore keep the 'family' atmosphere about the business. Two new factories were immediately commissioned. Recently, American Foods merged with Haskyns – another American multinational – to become Haskyns Foods, and since then, overseas control of Parker's has increased, to the dismay of long-serving managers.

The decision to merge was, of course, made in the United States, but has particular consequences for Parker Foods due to a tightening of overseas control. There is now 'interference' on management job-grading and pay; patenting procedures; the imposition on Parker's of another company's distribution function; tighter restrictions on capital spending; and there is now some monitoring of the job descriptions of directors, etc.

Parker's evolution from a small family undertaking into a large manufacturer, owned and controlled from the United States, is inscribed on the present organisation and management. This is dramatised in the differences between the new and old schools.

The old school are, by definition, long-serving. They have worked closely alongside members of the family board, as well as with (what was then) a small workforce. It was possible, insist the old school, to be on first-name terms, and they are alive to the intimacy of small-firm management and worker relations that this implied. This idyll gives them their clear conception of how a company should be run.

Some old schoolers feel the new 'outsider' managers have less loyalty to Parker's. Referring, for instance, to one new director, an old schooler says: 'He is a nice enough man, but somehow not in Parker's image.' And referring to the splitting of another director's job with the arrival of the new production director, he said that 'I would have thought there was no necessity for change . . . with the new plant.' There was 'no shame', he felt, in directors knowing the organisation right down to the shopfloor, to the nuts and bolts.

The old school believe that managers' responsibilities should reach to the shopfloor; that they should have personal obligations to both the company and the workforce; that they should train understudies, inculcating these values; that they should stand up and fight the union when challenged; that the parent company should leave Parker's managers' autonomy intact, etc. The new school, on the other hand, are younger, career-orientated and mobile and therefore, say the old school, do not show the same sense of moral obligation, either to the workforce or to the company. Their jobs are more rigidly defined and specialised. They are also inclined to take a different approach to the fact of union power, notably seeking to attach workers to the company through a human relations approach. However, the new schoolers describe themselves as 'people people', arguing that *their* approach is the moral one.

Again ironically, the old school, in conjunction with a firm of consultants, have helped write the job descriptions of the new school, which they now see as a force apart from them. As we shall see in detail later, the new school approach to labour management is in part a response to a rejection of the old school's 'high-handed' approach by the workforce. Unionisation was under way by the early 1970s, and by the mid-1970s the union was strong enough to launch their first strike. In answer to union pressure, the new school approach is to re-create workforce identification with the company rather than the union.

The stage of development of Parker's industrial bureaucracy is probably typical of British companies, whereas Harveys is more antiquated. The way it manages its social policies is probably also typical and, on black labour, similarly more progressive than Harveys. For this reason Parker's is presented as the second of our case studies.

CURRENT ISSUES

Parker's is inclined, as its managing director put it, to 'treat the outside world like the weather'. It has a similar *ad hoc* approach to internal issues, dealing with questions of social policy as and when they arise. These have usually occurred within the ambit of production and personnel functions. Social policy questions are treated in isolation from one another, in sharp contrast to the fourth of our case studies, where social policies are orchestrated under one guiding house 'philosophy'. Thus, our presentation of the issues here one by one, reflects the way the company manages them.

BLACK LABOUR

As in the case of Harveys, primarily for 'economic reasons' and in particular in response to labour shortages at the time, large numbers of black workers have been employed. At Parker's this has been especially Asians, a high proportion of these being female and having been employed from the early 1960s onwards. Since then the company has expanded consistently throughout the 1960s and 1970s, and the Asian workforce has expanded with it, family connections traditionally being important in recruitment. Today Indian labour accounts for the majority of the workforce, most of them being of Punjabi or Gujerati origin.

Unionisation came to the firm in the early 1970s, and a closed shop was negotiated ten years later. There is only one recognised union at Parker's, although there is a separate branch representing the lorry drivers. The main branch is run by Asian stewards, the transport branch by white. Until about a year ago maintenance engineers, who are virtually all male whites, were in the union, but they are now separately represented. According to the managers who have commented on this splitting off from the union, the reasons were firstly that the general union's policy is egalitarian and committed to the reduction of differentials. Secondly, unlike Harveys, the union here is consciously Asian. The union was set up by a long-serving Hindu. He was at one point dismissed for his militancy, but was reinstated. Recently he has been replaced by a Muslim. Shop steward elections are themselves something of a mystery to the white workers, having some of the characteristics of parliamentary elections, *vis-à-vis* the similarities of opposed camps to political parties. At the last elections there were three groups, one of which won the most important posts, gaining the positions of senior shop steward, branch chairman and branch secretary. The grounds for membership of, and patronage to, these camps are related in complex ways to personalities and to politics. And because of both differentials and black consciousness, the maintenance workers wanted separate bargaining rights. With only one maintenance steward among twenty or so Asian stewards, they thus felt they 'couldn't get a word in'. The company gave maintenance engineers staff status, offering to recognise a second union provided that the support of 80 per cent of *all* staff grades could be gained. The alternative management position is that maintenance could return to the hourly paid grades, and be recognised through the Transport and General. If two unions were recognised, senior managers were nevertheless afraid that there might develop a situation of 'leapfrogging'.

With respect to traditional trade union concerns – pay, conditions, manning levels, etc. – the union has been very successful at Parker's; but in addition, a consciously black – mainly Asian – workforce has taken an interest in negotiating a system of unpaid leave for visiting relatives abroad, in an assessment system for promotion to supervisory positions, and in industrial language training.

Asian workers are seen by managers to bring distinct cultural values to work. Thus some managers have suggested that there are 'ethnic problems' relating to hygiene and eating habits; attempted bribery pertaining to overtime and gaining employment; splits between the Singhs and the Patels; and other divisions along lines of age, sex, caste and religion, as well as between first- and second-generation Indians.

There have been several responses to the problems posed by a workforce which is both black and militant. Initially, the company discussed at senior management level the possibilities of 'balancing' the racial composition of the workforce. The 1968 Race Relations Act originally contained a Racial Balance Clause which legalised discrimination in order to 'disperse' concentrations of black labour. This clause was used by many employers in the late 1960s who had come to believe that 'concentration means trouble'.[1] The senior management committee considered canvassing 'known white areas' of the city at the same time as recruiting white European labour.

A move to produce more detailed employee records was ultimately rejected by the workforce on the suspicion that the company was seeking information on race. In any case, Parker's was overtaken by changes in legislation which removed the Racial Balance Clause from the 1968 Act. (The company is preparing, if forced by government, to compile a survey directly on the question of race.) By the late 1970s, 'dispersal' had been forgotten, and other means of managing union pressure and the Asian labour force were being sought. Accepting changes in the law and black militancy and some of the complexities of Asian shopfloor politics as facts of industrial life, Parker's considered new avenues, which included industrial language training, an assessment system and (less importantly) an attempt to extend company sports and social activities.

The company first looked into a system of industrial language training, with the help of the local (government-sponsored) Industrial Language Training Unit (ILTU). The ILTU have now been teaching at Parker's for several years. They have conducted various sixty-hour courses in the company, and these have included some teaching for managers in the problems posed by differences of language and culture in industry, as well as English language courses for workers. For managers 'industrial language training' concerns 'advanced communication training'. The objective is not necessarily to eliminate all cultural mannerisms, but to train managers to come to terms with them as socially normal and not see them as offensive. Thus video training is given in order to teach managers that the etiquette of communication among Asians is different, and not intended to be as brusque as may appear to be the case. The ILTU makes charges for its courses, though these are minimal, since the state pays 90 per cent of the costs.

It is especially worth noting that when we questioned ILTU members on their perceptions of Parker's management, they said that they too recognised an old school and a new school, and suggested that the new school were more receptive to language training needs. The personnel manager, they said, was instrumental in setting up language training. According to the ILTU, Parker's is 'tuned-in' to language training, and indeed industrial training in general. Successive interviews with the new school managers confirm that they are more inclined towards modern human-relations management (a point which will become clear during our discussion of the introduction of new technology), and therefore more receptive to the idea of communications training for managers and workers. Two personnel managers we spoke to were, indeed, particularly sensitive towards, and personally interested in, the culture and traditions of the Asian labour force.

While industrial language training is partly a response to state pressure, the assessment system is more to do with union pressures. In the early 1960s, black workers came to Parker's largely without industrial skills and often with little English language ability. They thus moved into the least skilled jobs, and there was consequently a strong demarcation between them and the skilled workers and foremen. Today there are still only a handful of black supervisors. Unlike Harveys, where the promotion of blacks has apparently never been a union issue, at Parker's the union has since its inception consciously sought a direct involvement in promotion procedures. For the union this is to a significant extent a black issue, while for managers it was seen initially as a question of managerial prerogative. According to the managing director, this issue came to a head a couple of years ago when a shopfloor worker who had failed in several job applications for supervisory grades complained that he felt discriminated against. In discussion with the managing director, a personnel manager recommended the establishment of a formal structure to assess shopfloor workers aspiring to management. The managing director said it was 'not necessarily for holy reasons alone', but 'to avoid future conflict'. the meritocratic assessment system which management wished to introduce – to be applied only to selected workers – has not totally satisfied either the trade union or many of the production line managers. Personnel managers had several objectives in mind. First, as stated, management wished to avoid accusations of discrimination. Secondly, by selectively applying the assessment system, management hoped to both discourage repeated applications by 'unsuitable' workers, and to encourage those with potential to apply. Thus, on the one hand, a manager said that it was 'to stop people forever applying for jobs. We "assess" them – the hard part is telling them.' Another manager said:

> Look, you know and I know that ninety per cent of the people on the shopfloor just haven't got it in them to be supervisors. But the union want assessment for the lot. Some of them don't even know what assessment is about, and I think they might even be frightened by being 'assessed'.

On the other hand, 'it's a problem to get certain people to apply for these jobs. We know we have the people with the capabilities, but they don't always apply.' The third objective is to invite workers to adopt the values of a meritocracy at the expense of cultural traditions of obligation to family and community: 'It would be a problem to Parker's that they might be more racially-inclined than Parker's management-inclined . . . there's a little bit of orientation towards India.' The union, he said, believes that some workers may be frightened of the prospect of rejection by subordinates at work who may, indeed, be their peers outside work. But many machine operators today, he said, were well educated, some having degrees, so the capability is obviously there. The fourth objective is to satisfy production managers and foremen that these capabilities *are* there – many production managers underestimate Asian workers.

The new assessment system has come up against two problems. For the union it does not go far enough. The activists demand that if the system is used at all, it is used to 'assess everyone', not just a select few. At the same time managers have suggested that the Asian workforce, in general, 'would prefer their relations to be promoted'. Also, according to management, the union would like to play the part in promotion that the assessment system was specifically introduced to avoid. The union is thus torn between a fully meritocratic 'Western' system and an 'orientation towards India'. Any reluctance on the part of potential managers on the shopfloor to apply for promotion is both because of the traditional antagonism of unions and management, and because of ethnic group loyalties. This is in addition, of course, to the tension between, on the one hand, loyalty to the union and, on the other, the union's would-be participation in finding new managers. The non-promotion of black workers is thus not a simple question of racial discrimination, but is overlaid by broader questions of prerogative. The existence of competing political patronage systems on the shopfloor again poses difficulties in promotion.

The other problem for the assessment system is production management: for them, the new system goes too far. Traditionally, as in Harveys, middle managers on the shopfloor have recruited their own supervisors and lower managers. The new system would, therefore, be an imposition. Personnel has so far failed to impose the system. A personnel manager joked: 'Assessment scheme? What assessment scheme?' In practice, production managers have retained the last say in promotions. The system is that a candidate fills in an application form, and gives it to his or her immediate supervisor, as was previously the case. This goes through the production manager, and only then comes to the personnel department, which then compiles a short-list. The relevant production manager and line manager next select from the list, and there is a second interview. In one or two cases, Personnel have stood their ground and applied aptitude tests to promising Asian candidates, in order to give them legitimacy. But so far assessment has mostly been limited to the three months' 'evaluation period' which a candidate goes through *after* he has been appointed. Personnel management have suggested that two Asian senior shop stewards would have made good managers, not least because they would have 'carried their people with them'. However in one case the shop steward's loyalties to his workforce were too great and, in the other, production management 'just wouldn't wear this at all'. Meanwhile, 'lots of complaints about lots of appointments' continue, and personnel managers still complain that the opinion held of Asians by some production managers is 'very difficult to get rid of'.

Most recently, with the opening of a new factory, an opportunity for promoting Asians into an expanded management team is being missed. In the past, management at

Parker's has been internally generated with growth. The union continues to insist on preserving 'management from within'. However, although the majority of over fifty recent staff and management appointments (many at the new plant) have been internal promotions, only a handful have been Asian. (Even this is a better record than at Harveys.)

With the best of intentions, both Personnel and the Industrial Language Training Unit have faced great difficulties in their new approach to the question of the management of a black labour force.

Finally, attempts to integrate Asians into the social life of the company have successively failed. The latest was a planned new sports and social club, to be generously financed by the company. Company-organised entertainment is now generally recognised as having been a failure, notably because sometimes Asians did not participate – having their own sense of community – while at other times only the men or the women participated. (In contrast, the white sections of the workforce do participate.)

Parker's is a definite advance on Harveys, in that both the union and progressive managers have put race relations on the agenda. *There is no criticism implied in the above statement of the real difficulties facing all parties*; however, progress remains slow.

NEW TECHNOLOGY

The union was strong enough by the mid-1970s to launch their first strike. This strike was over new technology. At that time Parker's opened a new factory with manning levels recommended by the Work Study department. These they set lower than at the old factory.

However, the union would not accept their findings, demanding manning levels more comparable to those at the existing plant, with its more antiquated machinery. After a three-day strike, the company acceded, compromising the Work Study team. Some middle managers feel 'sore' about senior management's 'sell-out' to this day. Work Study collapsed as a result, so that now it is used very little.

Another indication of shopfloor power concerned the introduction of a new machine at the warehouse, designed in consultation with the machine supplier in order to speed up van-loading times. This conveyor could be directed into the trailers more efficiently than under the previous system. To their surprise, however, its implementation resulted in no change in productivity. A manager explained what happened:

> When we introduced it, it improved turnaround and lessened the load on the loaders. But they don't load any more than they did before . . . they're delighted! It saves a lot of backache. We learnt a lesson: we didn't discuss with the men what we wanted, and it was too late once it was in. Yes, they have spare time now. What's happened is that their work rate is reduced.

Thus the new school are seeking new ways of managing, whilst the old school report that they look on with a degree of resignation. However, according to one new schooler, the 'dictatorial' tradition is still well entrenched. He explained that consultants had been working in the production department for years, trying to bring in new thinking, even though their training schemes cost 'an absolute fortune', and meant 'going through the same thing all the time . . . it's a long haul'. The prescription offered is for 'people people rather than machine people'. But, this manager stated, they are largely reduced to replacing managers as they leave, after a 'long, long time' of attempted change. This struggle between the old and new schools has come to a head with the introduction of new technology to the latest new plant. This new factory (opened recently) represents a major investment, and will replace an existing factory and massively increase capacity in future. The new technology introduced includes several major innovations, incorporating electronic controls, most of which increase labour productivity. The engineering director was responsible for procuring the new machinery. However, before start-up, this old schooler was 'promoted sideways', with the divorce of the engineering function from the production function.

The new production director is an ex-consultant to Parker's, and a new schooler. He had been previously involved in drawing up training schedules for production managers, and was made responsible for the whole production function, including the start-up of the new plant. The old schooler's displacement was reportedly to do with the sensitive state of shopfloor industrial relations. It was resolved that a new management strategy towards new technology had to be adopted for such an important investment.

The new school have, however, been forced to recognise the need for a 'softly, softly' approach both in respect to their old school colleagues and towards the shopfloor. The latter involves applying 'human relations' to new technology and work organisation. The new production director is the central figure here.

On displaced labour, the objective is to avoid redundancies and therefore appease the union. This has involved the extensive use of temporary labour at the factory, which is to be phased out so that as the labour-saving effects of the new technology become manifest, temporary labour will bear the brunt. The union has so far failed to unionise temporary labour, and thus extend its control in this area so, again reportedly, this is the only remaining opportunity for a 'high-handed' management approach. Significant here is the decision to *gradually* introduce new automatic packing and weighing machines which will replace a whole grade of labour. Although technically feasible at the new plant, full automation has been delayed. Instead, individual labourers will be displaced one at a time so that, through natural wastage and redeployment, mass redundancy can be avoided.

On the reorganisation of work, the central strategy is to develop 'line and shift solidarity', under which the remnants of Work Study has a new role. Work Study now gathers and analyses various production data for feedback to line managers and their 'teams'. The objective is to persuade workers to identify with their particular line, and to compete with each other line by line. This is intended both to increase output and to decrease union identification, for it is anticipated that management can now 'communicate' directly to line teams without going through shop stewards. In order to achieve line solidarity, integral teams have been made up by changing women's shift patterns. Formerly, women worked fixed shifts but they will now work alternating day shifts, as do the men. Teams will thus be kept intact week by week, and retain the same supervisors.

At the same time a 'key operator' scheme has been introduced, though against opposition from some shop stewards. The intention is to reduce overtime working by creating a flexible pool of readily available semi-skilled labour. Absenteeism will no longer demand overtime working, and thus is abolished what management believes is a root problem of industrial relations. The reduction of overtime is an objective shared with the district official.

These moves to 'motivate' workers are problematic not only because of resistance from some sections of the labour force, but also because of resistance from old school managers. Part of the production director's strategy for solidarity was to recruit site managers, readily identifiable with each plant. However, at the new plant the former production director managed to influence the selection of a new site manager so that an old schooler (not unlike himself) was recruited. The new site manager was thus ambivalent towards the *new* production director's thinking. On motivating the workforce, he expressed contradictory opinions. On the one hand he is favourable to a human relations approach. It makes 'people trust each other more – something which we haven't got here. There's a great deal of distrust on the shopfloor.' But he then says, 'sometimes I think we should just go back to saying, "Look, eight hours [work] is not a long time really, so why should we bother?" People can find their interests outside Parker's. It's not our business, even if jobs are boring and meaningless.' His attitude towards the provision of information line by line is again cynical. Referring to the remnants of Work Study, he commented: 'We have non-producers in our place . . . three girls . . . producing historico-statistics [shrugs shoulders].' And again, his ambivalence was apparent on the question of persuading line managers to accept team organisation:

> We've got a lot of training to do, of supervisors and managers first, to get a change in attitude [New School]. But sometimes I think you'd be better off going back to basics and jumping on people . . . we're down to thirty-eight hours a week . . . it's boring, mundane, no interest in it . . . there's no point in us trying to make it interesting for the short time they're here [Old School]. We haven't got enough line managers and supervisors who think. . . . They tend to be blinkered in their thinking . . . They don't think about doing something new . . . they sort of come in and stick to the same old ways [New School].

While a major investment has impressed upon management

the need for maximum utilisation, and thus persuaded them to seek new ways of motivating the workforce, the new shopfloor régime has not been directly determined by the technology itself. Rather, as with black labour, much more important in understanding social policy at Parker's is, on the one hand, managers' response to union power and, on the other, a continuing conflict between old and new schools of management. Management strategies thus result from what may be termed political processes.

EXTERNAL RELATIONS

The reader may be familiar with similar issues relating to black labour and new technology, from a knowledge of other firms. Parker's managers' response is probably not untypical in Britain. As we shall now also show, Parker's also conforms to the post-war corporate norm in its external relations. Unlike the issues of new technology and black labour, where the company had been forced to react to real internal and external political pressures, its external relations are largely voluntary. There is little overt pressure on the company here, and external relations are not seen as an object of management. As the managing director put it: 'We treat the outside like the weather.' As above, we here offer Parker's as an ideal typical case, to be contrasted with Pedigree Petfoods and other well-known corporations where external relations *are* seen as falling within the management prerogative, and where a very considerable financial commitment has been made.

The managing director at Parker's has laid down the guideline that the company should support only local charities and organisations. Beyond this, there is no policy. There is no external relations budget as such, though charitable donations which appear in the managing director's 'miscellaneous' budget reach several thousand pounds per annum, reported the finance director. He reflected the consensus at Parker's by adding that there is no recognised financial or other 'pay-off' from corporate donations, nor from managers' involvement in other local institutions and organisations; yet, he added, they had at least to take a company view of allowing *individual managers* to participate as they wished. These involvements were intuitive and moral rather than financial judgements.

Most managers and directors have few, if any, active memberships of city organisations and, with the exception of the Young Enterprise Scheme, participate only in their own time. The widely reputed 'pressure of work' and non-local residence is often given as an explanation by managers at Parker's for their relatively low activity here, just as it is by managers at probably the great majority of British companies.

The 'enlightened' personnel manager was indeed very critical of over-involved firms. We had come a long way since Cadbury's Bournville, he said, adding that his view of a plural society was, in fact, *incompatible* with corporate local domination. Comparing Parker's with our fourth case-study firm's known heavy involvement at Melton, he felt that this would be tolerated only during the depression, not under good economic conditions. He scorned, as he put it, 'living in a Cadbury's house, driving a Cadbury's car, getting buried in a Cadbury's coffin and doing a Cadbury's job'.

While two site managers were attempting to re-start Parker's sports and social club, the personnel manager doubted whether it would be supported: people 'just don't relate' to companies that way any more, he said. Pointing out that even now they had a sister Haskyns company in the city, which shared the same labour market but also lacked a social club, there was no possibility of combining to share facilities. Apparently, therefore, though the collective resources are there, the commitment is lacking on the part of both managers and workers.

Managers could get involved in parent-teacher associations, 'local political groups', the Boy Scouts, etc., but tended to do so in their *own* communities, he stressed, not in the city. He continued: professional and managerial people do not have time, nor did they *seek* the time to do district council politics, for attention to work came first, with perhaps participation in a professional association second. He confirmed, too, that though officially a member, the company was represented in person at the Chamber of Commerce only very occasionally. He agreed that community involvement had more generally declined as the welfare state had developed. 'We take the view that we're in business to make money.' While supportive of local charities, this support tends to be financial rather than through direct personal participation. A personnel officer listed aid to the city council for Voluntary Services, Age Concern, membership of the Food Manufacturers Federation Industrial Liaison Section, contact with the county council's Educational Industrial Liaison Officer, and the Young Enterprise Scheme (YES) and a small-business promotion scheme. The personnel officer is an official on the YES area board (see below).

Substantively, the county council's Educational Industrial Liaison Officer had invited Parker's personnel officer to give talks about industry to schools, an invitation which had been accepted. This manager holds a grievance about standards of literacy in school-leavers, but did not use such a link to make representations on this, as Petfoods might well have done in this situation. Parker's declined to have school visits to the company. The personnel department has arranged Industrial Society lectures at Parker's and was, as we saw, responsible for 'liaising' with the area Industrial Language Training Unit.

Personnel managers' local connections are probably greater than the majority of the company's managers, who more typically will be restricted to active or passive membership of professional associations. One or two directors are members of a local small-business scheme, but the company's contribution has been financial and passive rather than active.

Contacts with the local authority do exist, and like Personnel's relationship with the Industrial Liaison Officers, these tend to be informal but 'businesslike' and particular to the relevant functions. For example, town planners were contacted only after Parker's had decided to set up the new site. It was not the case of a liaison being cultivated, as with Petfoods and the planners, although in this case a respondent did instance the relationship at Parker's by reference to a telephone call to a member of the local planning department over the details of a planning consent: they were on first-name terms, and solved the problem between them over the telephone.

It is no good trying to threaten, force or manipulate planners, a director pointed out; although he found planners were not as brisk as were managers in industry, they did have a 'working relationship' on the basis of this understanding. When Parker's had tried to bring pressure to bear on the council over a planning application, and proposed to leave the area altogether, the planners did not respond. This position again contrasts strongly with our fourth case-study firm, which cultivates a close relationship with the planning authorities. It thus seems that Parker's is not a participant in any informal local élite in civic life. It would see little to gain from attempting to further its interests in this way, and it is probable that no cohesive business–civic élite actually exists in the city.

The evidence for this came from our examination of the Young Enterprise Scheme[2] and the local small-business advice scheme. The important feature was that the managers associated with each project had generally not previously met each other. This applied even to the chairmen of the city's first and third largest manufacturers! A new business–civic network of sorts was being created. However, this was very informal, largely restricted to younger junior and middle managers, and did not yet have a coherent set of élite values to identify it. Clearly, part of the explanation for Parker's non-involvement in external relations is that there is, indeed, no already-existing circle of notables in the city in which to participate. Parker's financially supports both initiatives mentioned above, though only a handful of managers choose to participate actively. Both the YES and the business scheme have fairly narrow objectives.

Parker's relationship with its suppliers is similarly unexceptional, though it is worth pointing out that the present 'gentlemanly' relationship with suppliers may be becoming increasingly bureaucratised. Under American influence, a supplier-assessment scheme has been systematically implemented for certain raw materials. Similarly, there is some pressure from new schoolers within the company to regulate their suppliers' practices. However, the old school directors responsible for supplies have so far resisted the application of 'scientific' principles in the choice of suppliers, preferring a more personal and informal relationship. As one old schooler pointed out, although he welcomes some of the experiments of the technical department, he feels that:

> this is not the be-all and end-all. I welcome assistance – technical guys coming in. But we must never assume that we can write a manual. There are things we have no control over. . . . It's much better to manage through loyalty and respect.

Finally, the company is faced with an effluent problem and regulation by the local water authority. The company has attempted until recently to treat its own effluent. This has largely failed, and Parker's has been forced to pay the water authority for the responsibility of final treatment. Parker's has found the original 'gentlemen's agreement' with the authority to be increasingly strained, as the authority demands a rising rate of charges. A manager complained that 'they've got us screwed down'. Again, the contrast with Pedigree Petfoods on this issue is striking.

SUMMARY

While Parker's management has had no choice but to respond to workforce-related issues over the past ten years, managers have been able to remain largely unconscious of their position on external relations. On workforce issues, the union has been influential in creating an agenda to which management has chosen to react in various ways. On external relations, there has been very little social and political pressure on the company, a minor exception being their relationship with the water authority. Otherwise, managers are left to their own devices. The company is largely irrelevant as a point of reference for the community activities. Having been established in the 1950s, Parker's was never involved with the provision of paternal services to employees and the local community, as these were already the defined political responsibilities of the welfare state. This historical context explains why the company has been able to 'treat the outside world like the weather'. With its recent involvements in the local small-business and Young Enterprise schemes, conceivably reflecting a change of mood in British political economy, and with a rising new school in the process of formation, conscious choices *may* be made towards a political role for the firm. However, these involvements are tentative, and there is little evidence to suggest that they might become more extensive. Other firms in the city are also little involved, and there is no coherent business–civic élite.[3]

In our next case study, a long-established firm, with a paternal–autocratic tradition dating back to the nineteenth century, has indeed made a conscious decision to extract itself from public life and bring itself more into line with a Parker's-like approach. This makes our final case study all the more significant for, alone in our researches, it claims to take the view that there are private solutions to public problems.

Workforce-related issues at Parker's have taken a different course. Here, a strong and consciously black union has, since the early 1970s, made various demands of management. We illustrated the political strength of the union by reference to new technology and to equal opportunity at work. As we saw, the response of management depended on its culture and 'political anthropology'. A confrontational approach among older managers, originally schooled in an autocratic–paternal tradition of family management, was giving way to a new generation who have drawn on the human-relations approach advocated by the contemporary business schools. They saw this as a practical alternative where the old school approach had been compromised. The battle for ascendancy is still being waged.

5 'It's a National Government Problem, not Ours'

Davis's Foundry is wholly owned by a continental multi-national. Previously, the company was autonomous, and was privately owned and controlled by the Davis family until the mid-1960s. Established some one hundred and thirty years ago, it is the oldest of our case-study companies. The company has had other interests duing its long history but is now principally known as a general foundry. Turnover for the last financial year was over £25m., representing an upturn in the company's fortunes after major redundancies spread over several years. Less than 700 are now employed.

The foundry is sited in an industrial town in the Midlands, whose growth has depended in considerable part on the fortunes of the company. With the nationalisation of its coal-mining interests and the introduction of new technology and rationalisation, the proportion of the town's labour force employed by the company declined. However, despite this, and the foundry's much reduced scale, it remains a relatively important local employer.

The company still has a lingering local reputation for business welfarism, having provided housing, health care, a church, schools and recreational facilities. Today, however, these institutions are no longer the company's responsibility, and contact between senior managers and the town has largely withered away in comparison with the past. Remaining contacts are of a rather different nature, thus ending a long tradition of heavy involvement in the town's life by the Davis family, as we shall see.

Shortly we shall describe managers' more recent experience of these radical changes in company social policies. First, however, we shall list some aspects of the company's current practice on several issues.

CURRENT ISSUES

Ownership by a foreign company brought the imposition of Davis's *Environmental Plan*. This, feel local management, might partly reflect the stringency of continental environmental planning legislation experienced at headquarters. The company had begun to develop an environmental policy prior to the takeover, but takeover meant a *formal* budget on environmental planning and the development of laid-down guidelines and objectives. In the period 1980–5, it was planned to spend about £1m. on various projects intended to improve the local environment and working conditions, this representing an advance which does not, of course, necessarily quantify all the many improvements which the progressive introduction of new technology has brought incidentally.

Many of these changes are, nevertheless, responses to the implementation of United Kingdom legislation. For instance, new legislation proposed no noise, which would considerably reduce permitted decibel values, will require the company to spend significant sums in suppressing noise in their plants even to approach the new limits. Similarly, the company is working to comply with reports received from the factory inspectorate on a range of health and safety issues, although here the relationship is described as reasonable and amicable. There has never been a banning order. Other aspects of the plan are purely voluntary. For instance, the company's plan to 'beautify' the works is a response to neither the community nor to the workforce itself, and is only remotely to do with pressure from public authorities.

Over the past fifteen years or so, there have been several hundred redundancies. As we shall see, the company feels that it is in no position to be responsible for unemployment in the area. The company is, however, anxious to keep intact the skills and knowledge of its labour force, and has recently used available government grants helping them retain at least some redundant labour, which might otherwise have been lost.

Since much of this chapter is on the *changing nature of company social policies*, the emphasis will be as much on what has been given up as on current practice, and the reason for this. This emphasis has been decided upon because we feel Davis's is an ideal-typical example of an experience undergone by countless companies. It thus establishes an historical benchmark for the policies reported in our other case studies, and a strong indication of the fate of business welfarism.

TRANSITION

The first view of the town itself is dominated by the foundry, which fills a valley floor. On one side of the valley is the parish church, a legacy of nineteenth-century paternalism, which stands overlooking the company which largely funded it.

On the other side of the valley lies the town itself. For most of its history it has been a one-company town. The paternalism of the company's founder continued in a steadily diluted form up to the end of private ownership. The generation of manager who came on the demise of the family are critical, describing the previous régime as 'autocracy with little professiona management or delegation'.

In management terms the family's retreat had begun some fifteen years before the takeover as the board appointed non-family directors. Respected 'outsiders' were brought in who began to institute changes which, the Davises stated might otherwise have been unacceptable to them. Consultant were also employed on a number of projects, technical and financial, including diversification and rigorous rationalisa-tion. Most important of all, financial advice was taken which convinced the family that the company would have to go public if death duties were to be avoided, and in order that capital be recovered on behalf of the family's overseas branches. Given the family's history at the company, this was a traumatic change to contemplate; however their consent was secured and city agents were retained to implement the transition in status to a public limited company.

The style of management changed particularly rapidly in 1970, when the first of a new generation of managers was brought in. The present managing director came at this time. The situation in the early 1970s was seen in the following terms.

Productivity was low; in many sections of the plant the buildings, equipment and methods needed modernisation; there was unnecessary handling – including manhandling; the overall impression was of outdated plant, insufficient capital investment and a straggling, poorly-planned site. Despite the poor physical and working conditions, there were few com-plaints from the workforce – who generally thought conditions were much better than twenty years before. Almost 70 per cent of the workforce had over ten years service, and many over twenty years. Rates of pay were low and the payments system complicated. Communications within the company were poor;

there was some harking back to the settled 'good old days' of the Davis family as opposed to the more remote and frequently changing new management. There was also mistrust of management arising from redundancies and non-replacement of natural wastage, which created anxiety and insecurity.

The new school of managers might be described as 'robust' and 'professional'. However they are not insensitive on the relationship with either the town or their own employees. As one of the new generation of managers explained, the company faced something of a dilemma:

New technology always aims to engineer people out. Machines are very much more predictable than people, and secondly, various things government has done to protect the interests of people have militated against. For example, if we can have machinery that will work with fewer people, it's very much easier to switch it on and off according to demand. People, on the other hand, have rights – you can't pull the plug out on people. We quite clearly aim to engineer people out of our company. I believe, on a personal level, that the next big industry must be leisure. It's a national government problem, *not ours*.

Honestly and truly, our problem here is not to think about what to do with 3.9 million unemployed on the streets. We pay the government to look after that.

But,

Where there is a difficulty is that we're not lost in a big city . . . [We're in] a community. So, perhaps we ought to have a greater social responsibility than we have got. But it's undischargeable. We can't keep 50 more people on that we would otherwise be sending home.

71

Logically, he deduced, if the company followed an alternative policy, then it 'might not be around next year' as an operating concern.

It should be emphasised that this was *not* intended as callous reasoning. (Like most of the senior managers and directors at Davis's, his father worked in heavy industry.) The conclusion that the company is not responsible for unemployment is largely drawn from the fact that the state has accepted 'responsibility' for unemployment. It has been resolved to take public responsibility for those cyclical effects of the private economy.

While Davis's managers are unanimous that the foundry was in no position to do more than 'mind its own business', and that state responsibility was necessary, this did not prevent one manager from making a more negative assessment of state intervention. He felt that the local market was characterised by low productivity and a reluctance to seek work. The company had, until recently, a labour turnover problem which he explained in terms of high dole payments and a consequent reluctance to work. Such a dualist approach to the question of state goods and services is, of course, not untypical among managers: agreeing that private solutions cannot always be provided, yet pointing to the inefficiency caused by the state's activities. This line of complaint extends to the unreasonableness of limiting regulation, for example on noise.

It is interesting to contrast the preceding manager's view of obligation, rights and duty with those of Tom Davis and later family owners, as reflected in the evolution of the company.

Reputedly, Tom Davis and the family dynasty which inherited ownership and control of the company were 'mindful of the obligations as well as rights of ownership' and 'revered the industrial labourer'. Under them, the company provided variously schools, religious institutions, sponsored carnivals, clubs, societies and open days, health services (a surgery and

72

contributory health scheme, which ended with the advent of the National Health Service), houses and company farms. It is not difficult to detect autocratic motives in this, and social consent was a stated desired objective. Similarly, as one director pointed out, the way Tom Davis incorporated landed interests in the company, and bought out the farms beneath which he wanted to recover minerals, was an 'environmental policy' of a sort. This secured the consent, too, of the local aristocracy for the development of the company. These were private solutions to private problems.

In conceding that there were other interests than their own involved in the enterprise, the Davises were, perhaps, unconsciously anticipating the welfare state and its extension of public rights. With the state's assumption of these responsibilities, the political and civic role of the company's managers and directors was drastically reduced. This is what the manager quoted earlier refers to when he says that the company's social responsibility is 'undischargeable' and that the government is paid to look after it. Today's managers state a clear preference in favour of the new régime. As one long-serving senior manager recalled of the nineteenth-century paternalist inheritance: 'I must say I've been right through, and I prefer the new system really.' A paternal concern was offered or, more accurately, imposed: the Davis company sought loyalty in return for its paternal concern. But, he added,

They didn't expect to pay very much. . . . In the old days, nobody knew what anyone else was getting, and it was a case of having to ask for a rise. . . . Quite a lot depended on whether you were in the Territorials or not whether you [actually] got a job.

As stated, the company pits were nationalised in the late 1940s, but the Davis family retained control of the remainder of the company. Over a period of twenty years, it has gradually become this manager's responsibility to dispose of much of the rest, including company houses and a considerable agricultural acreage.

The company became a private limited company before the First World War. It was by going public in the mid-1960s that the fate of its managerial traditions and civic role was finally sealed. The Davis family, according to this same manager, had feared the effect of death duties, and were worried that they might have to sell off the whole firm if they had no capital behind them. In this way, the first overseas multinational was eventually able to take over the firm by share acquisition. Soon after the takeover, the last of the Davises resigned and the new owners began a swift purge of the old school managers reaching right down to the foreman level. The old autocratic paternalism, which was a personal, face-to-face style of managing was replaced by a system of management by objectives. This had been strongly advocated by overseas headquarters for its claimed rationality and therefore anticipated superiority to the old system.

CHANGING SOCIAL POLICIES

The new school apply a narrower definition of corporate obligation. However, probably because of a particularly high representation of managers and directors from working-class backgrounds, the organisational culture of the company is quite particular.

The new school appreciate the repressive side of paternalism. They repudiate it instinctively:

In the old days, you paid as little as you could and assuaged your conscience with . . . social do-gooding. People sneer at you as paternalist. I don't want to be called paternalist. What the Davises were doing was exemplary in the light of the situation *then*. *My* responsibility is to give guys their security . . . a wage, and then let him decide how to spend it. The old way was to pay as little as possible and then dole out soup to assuage the conscience. But most of the families had a sense of responsibility.

The point was, however, that the situation had been transformed: 'Every employee here is given a chicken at Christmas. Now, when it started, it was quite significant, but now I think it's a bit condescending and meaningless and I don't like it.' Even more significantly, this director was adamant in his criticism of Michael Heseltine's request that businessmen get 'reinvolved in the community':

I don't think managers have the time to participate in the community as he asks. And there are lots of things about community participation which I hate. For example, I despise the Rotary. When I first came, I noticed how all the reps had got a certain make of car, hardly the car for hard driving, so we set about finding out how this was the case and it turned out that there was a car salesman in the Rotary and he was probably doing business there. We put a stop to that. The whole thing was so bloody pathetic it made me cringe.

As for being involved in local government, that, he felt, would be even more inadvisable. 'It's dangerous for a company to get involved.' Managers were even wary of participation where a direct company interest could be envisaged. The company, he explained, had a tip where it dumped waste sand and, indeed, if the company had a representative director on the council, for example, then 'it might be much easier for us to operate the tip ... but it's beyond my thinking and the managing director's. We would never contemplate it'.

Relations with local authority officials were now 'businesslike' rather than informal, and could not be described as corporate involvement in the community. A remaining old school director pointed out that as county planners 'work to the letter of the law ... it does help in future (planning) applications if you develop a good record of restitution and so on'. This was more a question of building up a good record than bringing influence to bear. Even where this manager had given evidence for various bodies on Town and Country Planning, and made particular recommendations on behalf of the company, he feels that matters are often within the state's discretion. Often, 'the planners have made up their minds before they ask you,' he reported. Indeed, the conclusion that corporate local participation is, in contrast to the period of paternalism, actually damaging, has been reinforced in present managers. The company had been considerably embarrassed at having been accidentally implicated in a planning 'row' which reached the point of involving central government. The company was actively ensuring that the risk of a repeat would be obviated in future, by divesting itself of certain remaining community commitments.

Another director discussed the community at large: 'We are accused of being indifferent ... but would be accused of paternalism if we started going back in the other direction.' In civic life, the new school are represented sometimes in a personal, but never in a corporate capacity. Although one director felt that there might be direct gains from 'knowing the right people', he found the idea of behind-the-scenes operating quite distasteful, this being true even though a given interest might fall within the boundaries of his particular function.

The *Environmental Plan* is no exception to Davis's new pattern of involvement. This originated from the overseas parent, and is now managed routinely by Davis's managers, who see it neither as paternal benevolence nor intended as a means of bringing influence to bear on local authorities. If anything, workers see it as a luxury. The managing director commented: 'When we first started doing these sorts of things [we got comments like] "Why can't we have the bloody money?"'. Another director commented that 'tree planting is not noticed locally'.

Significantly, the environmental plan is based on *laid-down* objectives for management in the *Manual of Management by Objectives* drawn up by overseas headquarters. 'Social responsibility' is included in covering the environmental plan. There are four 'unit objectives'. Such detailed specification would, of course, have been quite alien to the implicit, moral codes employed by the Davises under autocratic paternalism. Stated as unit objectives today are:

 (i) company image (with, as examples, public relations, plant appearance, compliance with influencing legislation;
 (ii) law;
 (iii) safety;
 (iv) environmental harmony (location of sites and operating procedures).

Customer and employee satisfaction, including health and safety, appear separately at other points on the list of objectives.

The contrast with the last family member's approach to obligation is indeed strong. Though not unconcerned at site appearance, the essence of 'social responsibility' lay elsewhere. He explained, in retirement, that in the days previous to the welfare state, his father and grandfather had seen it as a natural part of their role to 'help those who had fallen on hard times . . .

who came to their door'. He continued by explaining how, while autocratic paternalism might be anachronistic now, it was to the Davises quite natural at the time:

> Looking back, I feel that my feeling of tradition was exaggerated. . . . It is possible that the meaning of the word 'paternalism' rather provoked the other feeling. [But] we were *never* involved because we thought of it as doing people good; we were involved because we *lived* there. Pre-war, when there wasn't the social security, my predecessors felt they could do what they could to help. . . . I think it's very sad that owning families move away to the south of England, which means there just isn't the cross-fertilisation of ideas [between owners and the community].

LIMITS

Unlike Mr Davis who lived close to the foundry town, as had his ancestors before him, many of today's senior managers and directors live away from the works. Many do so deliberately. One director commented: 'If you live thirty miles away how the hell can you know the bloke in the back-to-back up the road from the works?' The sense of community which remains in the works town is no longer directly shaped by the company, as had previously been the case. The same director continued: 'Here, there's still very much of a mining village mentality. [But] I don't create it, I don't run it . . . they run it . . . it's from within.'

As well as living some distance away, being 'too busy' is also given as a reason for not participating. The few managers and directors who have tried to 'participate' recently have done so only in a deliberately limited sense: 'When somebody retires, that sort of thing.' Thus one manager sits on some local committees, as do other senior managers, but he says 'it's fairly trivial, really'. There are other instances of participation by managers in civic life, both in the town and in the wider region. However, the point is that their activities are essentially *personal*, not *corporate*, and do not carry anything like the significance which they would have carried under the Davises.

'Going too far' would complicate life, managers felt, and getting involved in local politics – the ultimate responsibility sought by the old dynasty – 'wouldn't be worth the aggro'. As one director put it, managers 'prefer not to get involved because it complicates matters considerably'. The chairman explained that the directors 'don't mind getting drafted – I am interested in the community and society – but neither they nor I would ever get involved on the stump of going round for votes every four years'. In his own external activities he is, for the most part, represented in a personal capacity only. Indeed, the new owners have tended to discourage extra-corporate activities. The chairman continued by agreeing that, like Davis's managers in general, he too is principally 'profit-accountable' to the others. Beyond that, he feels that headquarters need not be over-concerned with what he does externally. Finally, he added while *some* of his involvements *may* contribute towards private industry's collective lobby of Parliament, he felt they are no more than mildly influential. In those cases where a corporate benefit had been gained for Davis's, it appeared more a question of access to information through business forums rather than of corporate influence. Apart from having an effect on the public image of his company, he values these outside contracts for several reasons. For example, they keep him in touch with attitudes and wider issues, both formally and informally. Secondly, by making contacts through employers' organisations with chairmen of public industries, he is able to make strategic planning judgements, as a substantial part of his company's sales are under government contract. Thirdly, he is personally interested in the relationship between government and industry, being concerned about the quality of public-industry planning and the need to study the operation of the new mixed economic system which has developed, and which involves the integration of industry, government and public authorities.

Returning to the local level, another director fears that if directors became involved in *local* politics once more (even informally), it would make things difficult in industrial bargaining. This, he thought, must be free of any connotations of political ideology, and if directors were known to be 'ideological' then bargaining would be much more difficult to control. In this case, it is clearly not purely a question of managerial choice, but a recognition of the *strength* of the trade unions (which had not been as well placed during the Davis era). A third director agreed: 'Managers try not to be political if they can help it – it comes into industrial relations – they like to have discussions without politics coming into it . . . We feel we should not be partisan'.

Also, Labour control of the local council limits private influence in public affairs, and avoidance of the 'political question' lies behind much of the company's steady withdrawal from the local community. Anything beyond strictly limited *ad hoc* participation would be seen as 'too pushy . . . the locals wouldn't contemplate it'.

THE NEW RATIONALITY

For Davis's managers, the need to return profits is a matter of fact and not an intensely ideological question. For them this is

simply the way it is. The handful of old schoolers who have
survived accept this logic: if the company does not pursue
labour productivity, and if it refuses to contemplate redundancy, or is diverted into providing paternalistic services to its
employees, then it goes out of business.

While it may be, in practice, that the directors pursue
profitability as an objective, two of them also emphasised that
they were themselves employees of the company, and that they
thought of their work in terms of preserving employment as
much as in terms of making a profit. One said: 'I see the
company as a source of income and security [for the workers]
rather than of profit as the be-all and end-all of business'.
Although this perception of their own work may not actually
change the logic they pursue, it does, nevertheless, release them
from some of the personal contradictions that could be
expected of directors with working-class backgrounds. The
concept of working both for profit and to protect existing jobs
has an evidently reassuring clarity about it for such managers.
One director went so far as to state:

> We should have given employees rights in business. As you
> know, shareholders have the first share. People – hell –
> they've put a lot at stake . . . [Workers] have got to change.
> They don't want a say at board level. Their main aim is to
> achieve greater pay for the members by fighting the company
> instead of cooperating . . . the concept of the union doesn't
> allow for that, however. . . . Just keeping a job is almost
> sharing a business.

This identification with the workforce goes hand in hand
with their attitude towards the overseas owners. One senior
manager complains, 'Employees can't see that I am an employee too'. He added:

I don't know who I'm working for and frankly I'm not interested [in the owners]. I *do* see it as a matter of ensuring continuing work here and for the sons who want to come here. Our first responsibility is to be in business next year. A bit of hardship now is better than no company later . . . I say I know what's in the interest of these guys.

However, he is quite clear that he is not in a position to challenge corporate imperatives even if he were to choose to. He explains:

The guy who controls this company sits in an office abroad. We control with a small 'c', him with a big 'C'. Once we start running badly, then we'll see who's really in control. Within his parameters we do what we can. And anyone who thinks otherwise is kidding himself.

One manager emphasises the limits of his own discretion, returning to the theme that he is also but a managerial employee: in the old days of the Davises 'the directorship would have been family and friends. But employees are slow to get the message that directors are now employees too. Candidly, one of the points I readily make is "I work for a salary the same as you". But there is this mystique'.

The effect, understandable as we argue it to be, is that whilst its managers and directors are working-class and identify their interests with those of the company's employees, in practice they are further removed from both their own workforce and from the community at large. The manager explains: 'The old management would say, "Hello, Harry. How's Mabel?" and he'd be right – Mabel *was* his wife. The workforce nationally has moved away from the company. People don't involve themselves any more. They've moved away from their company for their social life.' And as we have made clear, a previous autocratic–paternal sense of corporate belonging has, in any case, been rejected by the new generation of managers.

Although working-class by allegiance, then, directors feel that they have burnt their bridges collectively, both with the 'community' and with their own workforce. This, explains a manager, despite that 'we're all from the working class round here'. And despite the fact that 'there aren't any dragons from Eton [amongst us]'.

There are some comments from one or two directors that suggest they would like to retain some of these bridges, but they seem unlikely to succeed. Some participate in certain local associations, make small donations to local clubs and charities, and preside over the works football team which draws players who need not work at the company. 'These things are trivial in a way,' said one director, 'but people do appreciate it. It's an opportunity to meet people. There's nothing more excruciating than walking around the shopfloor without knowing names.' Significantly, he is one of the directors who has decided to 'stay put', ending his 'gypsy-like' cosmopolitan career to date, and therefore having more of an opportunity to 'join in'. The managing director is also an exception to the rule, in that he seeks to involve himself in the community and with the workforce, and is one director who has chosen to live in the area. His account of this is as follows:

> The more I got involved, the more I wanted to do for the town. . . . Although the blokes didn't like it, they appreciated what I was trying to do [to save the foundry]. The majority would eventually see the writing on the wall, so basically that was one of the things that drove me on . . . it was a thankless task. They were pretty militant, but I got to know them; in fact I got to know more people than anybody.
>
> I was at the football match last night – I live fairly close by – something which I did deliberately . . . I know some of the

councillors and I like them – they're OK: good, solid citizens.
It's a mining village mentality here. They're very stubborn
. . . but I like them.

Asking him if he often met local Labour party activists, he
replied,

What do you mean, 'meet 'em'? I'm part of the community so
I *know* them. I don't have to go to look for them, they're here.
I deliberately live in the community. . . . Perhaps I can talk
to the people because I'm of the people. . . . You don't have
to agree with them to respect them.

I'm not just altruistic, I'm a real hard businessman – one
of the hardest, but I still think doing the things I've been
talking about help you get success – it's a double-sided coin.
'He's a hard bugger', they'll tell you, but I hope they'll say it
with a smile on their faces.

At the time of the changeover from the Davises, there was
a vacuum which needed to be filled to give peace of mind to
all our management and works employees. . . . Undoubtedly
there have been times . . . when personal contacts outside the
works environment have assisted in settling industrial
disputes, both with management unions and works unions.

For all this, his involvement has limits, and in any case the
company has seen a considerable turnround in managers since
the takeover, and therefore a turnover in people who never had
time to invest in the community. Doubtless, even the managing
director finds the majority of shopfloor workers strangers to
him, despite his intention to develop a more intense familiarity.
Indeed, he admits that: 'It is almost impossible to interest
directors and managers in this type of participation under
today's business climate.'

The Davis Company is directed by men on a post-war set of

ethics and political affairs. They are very probably correct in their belief that the company would have folded without the professionalism in management that the takeover produced, and of which they are an embodiment. Equally, they are correct in deducing that both older patterns of business welfarism outside the firm and autocratic paternalism within are no longer tennable in the town, as even the last of the Davises concedes. The welfare state, managers and trades unions repudiate the older system of industrial and local relations. Directors and managers affirm this, both as 'hard-headed businessmen' and on the basis of their own working-class origins.

They are close to the essence of social democracy in defining their responsibilities as being confined to the particular objectives of business in the last instance, and in recognising the state's role beyond. Although at a personal level they might like to judge themselves on the jobs they have secured by 'minding their own business', they freely admit that there are public problems that cannot be solved privately.

6 Mutuality of Benefits

Pedigree Petfoods is wholly-owned by Mars Inc., one of the largest private corporations in the world. As a deliberate policy, the operating units of the Mars Corporation throughout the world enjoy individual autonomy, and the headquarters staff, at McLean, Virginia, is remarkably small – less than half of one per cent of total employees.

The company enjoys about 50 per cent of the total United Kingdom prepared petfood market, and over 60 per cent of the most important sector of the market – canned dog and cat food. In 1982, its turnover, for the first time, exceeded £300m. By volume, the company averaged a 10 per cent per annum growth in output in the twenty-five years to 1977, and strong growth continues today, with gradually expanding dog and cat populations. (As well as this population increase, market research has shown a trend towards the convenience of feeding prepared petfoods and away from scraps and fresh meat.) Taking account of the relatively small size of the workforce (about 2000), these figures indicate an extremely high rate of productivity. At the main Melton Mowbray plant, production is in excess of $3\frac{1}{2}$ million cans of petfood per day, on a four-shift system (24 hours a day, 7 days a week).

The main canning works (established in 1951) is sited at Melton Mowbray, in the heart of rural Leicestershire –

population 23,554. Here, the company directly employs about 15 per cent of the town's total labour force, and many others are employed by supplying firms, especially transport contractors. Dry and semi-moist petfoods have, since the mid-1970s, been produced at a new plant at Peterborough – about 35 miles away. About 200 'associates' work at Peterborough. The National Office and the Animal Studies Centre are located at Waltham-on-the-Wolds, about 5 miles north-east of Melton.

The company operates close financial controls, and one of these measures is ROTA (Return on Total Assets). This is commonly known by Petfoods managers as 'getting the most out of your assets'. The company's central objective as defined by ROTA is to maximise return on total assets. In terms of food processing, packaging and marketing, Petfoods, with a heavy investment in food processing and packaging technology, is technologically among the most advanced in the world. Any aspects of production and distribution which can be considered peripheral are contracted out – this includes transport and engineering installations. One of the key performance measures for the company is the ROTA index, and pay rises and bonus payments, including those for directors, are linked to the ROTA performance.

Pedigree Petfoods has a reputation locally and nationally as a morally-concerned and ethically-responsible company. The people who know it as such include local clubs and societies, local authorities, the veterinary profession, animal scientists, breeders, animal-welfare societies, educationalists, and managers in other companies, to name just a few. It conveys the image of a caring and progressive employer – paying wages well above the local average, providing excellent working conditions, and being at the forefront in the UK on experiments in job design and work humanisation. It is a good neighbour to the local community in Melton Mowbray – putting time and money into local charities and social activities, ensuring that any problems to do with noise, smell and traffic movements are kept to a minimum, and more recently involving itself in a local venture to encourage small business. It even encourages the responsible ownership of pets – running the most advanced scientific centre in Europe for the study of pet animals, supplying educationalists with advice and teaching materials on responsible pet ownership, and advising local authorities on how best to deal with their dog populations.

This reputation is supported within the company under the guiding principles of Mutuality of Benefits. These are: 'a good deal for the housewife; a good deal for the associate; and a good deal for the trade'. These principles were derived in the 1930s by the Mars family, and are continually reviewed and instilled in Mars managers worldwide (of whom there are 3800). Recently, for instance, Mars conducted a world review of its managers' understanding of mutuality of benefits. Although these principles were incorporated in the setting up of Pedigree Petfoods, today's generation of managers and directors has developed the principle of mutuality in altogether new fields since the late 1960s. Internally, Petfoods has always offered favourable conditions of pay and employment, but it is only in the 1970s that it has further developed its mutual relationship with vets and breeders, educationalists, the local authority ,the local community and others. Each have a newly-perceived bearing on the company's affairs.

A unitarist understanding of mutuality of benefits is sustained by 'Open Management'.

OPEN MANAGEMENT

Both by reputation and in day-to-day practice, Pedigree Petfoods operates an open management system. Again part of the Mars design, managers, like production workers, clock on and off, share the same canteen and toilet facilities, and like all associates are formally of equal status. Petfoods managers have refined this open management system so that today there is far greater homogeniety of management approach, and an absence of managerial conflict. They achieve this through several means. First, recruitment and promotion criteria ensure a homogeneity of background and outlook – managers are likely to have come from the more prestigious universities, having had previous management experience in marketing-oriented companies. Secondly, senior managers are frequently rotated to prevent patronage systems within functions. Thirdly, managers are encouraged to articulate critical views and, conversely, are called on to defend their actions in open forum. This is expressed in terms of 'no doors on offices'; even the managing director works in an open-plan office. Again, this prevents secretive and subversive alliances forming. Finally, in order to be considered for promotion, a manager will have demonstrated an ability to cooperate with other managers. Intense competition for promotion thus actually encourages agreement on policy. As well as practising cooperation day-to-day, most Petfoods managers are trained to be consummate negotiators.

Having introduced the reader to some key aspects of the company, we shall now turn to a description of managers' own explanations of their social policies, to provide an understanding of this corporate morality from the inside.

PRESERVING INDEPENDENCE

Petfoods' strategy to incorporate workers in decision-making and in the design of work developed in the early 1970s, alongside labour unrest at the Melton plant, partly reflecting national dissent on Edward Heath's attempt to curb union power. Petfoods faced pressures for unionisation, despite the fact that the company already used a variety of means aimed at maintaining the loyalty and commitment of the workforce – a good pension scheme, relatively high wages, good working conditions, etc. At Parker's, as we saw, the parallel demand for unionisation was successful. At Petfoods, a system of consultative committees was set up by the management, which was intended to improve worker–management relations.

In 1973 and 1974 there were a series of spontaneous walk-outs which focused on pay, but they were also a symptom of difficult management–worker relations. In 1973, the current personnel director was recruited and was largely responsible for developing the company's response. ACAS were called in to arbitrate in the G & M's demand for bargaining rights at Petfoods, and on a ballot of the workforce this demand was rejected overwhelmingly. In the early days the committee system consisted of elected representatives of the workforce, and through these the company made a number of changes (for example, on shift bonuses). However, since then an apathy towards the system set in, and it has been abandoned in favour of a manager–employee briefing system.

Throughout the 1970s Petfoods was expanding at the same time as reducing the size of the workforce. A couple of years after the walk-outs, the first stage of plans for a programme of high automation was implemented. The associated 'Manpower Reduction Programme' was to mean several hundred jobs to go within a few years. To ensure the smooth introduction of the new technology, and to prevent the re-emergence of anticipated demands for unionisation, the consultative committee system was called into action to develop systems to handle the changes. Guarantees were given that labour displacement would be dealt with only through natural wastage and redeployment, and for those who remained came the prospect of higher grades (and thus higher wages) and job enrichment through new technology. Temporary labour, not covered by his commitment, was used to cushion the effects. Again, managers told us, this exercise was successful in preventing the re-emergence of demands for unionisation.

During this episode, according to one manager, some workers would try to use the committees as a 'bargaining' system rather than a 'consultative' system. In these cases, he felt, the exercise was 'a failure' – job enrichment should be about motivation and commitment to the company, not just a way of getting upgraded and paid more money. Nonetheless, job design was successful in many areas, and here there are now 'semi-autonomous work groups', with shared responsibilities, some of which previously belonged to technicians and supervisors. But the loyalty which management hoped to generate is continuously questioned, and indeed monitored, by the company. At the Peterborough plant, which manufactures packeted foods, the monitoring comes in the form of seven work group 'coordinators', whose job it is to assess the degree of autonomy that a work group can safely have. In some cases, autonomy has in fact been reduced. As one manager put it: 'They key problem is – do they have more short-term loyalty to the group or to the company?'

Another manager elaborated on the strategy at Peterborough. Peterborough was intended from the beginning as an organisational 'test-bed'. In consultation with the Tavistock Institute of Human Relations, Petfoods applied the concept of autonomous work groups. The objective was to implement a 'self-management' system to replace a system of 'robot jobs for which you had to pay extra if you wanted him to do anything else . . . it has broken down barriers, and the organisational experiment was a success'. Zone 7s, the 'coordinators', were introduced later for two main reasons. First, to provide a stepping-stone grade between workforce and management: 'We were able to offer a career step.' Secondly, 'if he [the supervisor] uses it [his position] properly, he can control the group without actually seeming to do so'.[1]

This manager related the experiment to the Bullock Report, the prevailing context of technically-induced redundancies, and the post-ACAS inquiry atmosphere. He emphasised, however, that 'you can regard job design as basically to get a more efficient system'. Finally, subject to technical differences between the Peterborough and Melton plants, the system of autonomous work groups is in the process of being transferred to Melton.

Thus, while being at the forefront of the international movement for the humanisation of work, managers are keen to point out that this is largely a means to more important ends – preserving managerial control, staying independent, increasing worker motivation, ensuring flexibility and reducing numbers humanely.

Although the focus of the research was on managers and corporate social policies, we felt it was important to hear a non-management account of the establishment and operation of the consultative system. Interviews were therefore arranged with two pairs of 'associates' who have been actively involved. What follows is their combined account, using their words.

In the 1950s, this company, like others, was autocratic, but the youth of the 1960s would not continue to accept it. They challenged it. People wanted to have a voice in things. *Ad hoc* meetings took place. These disrupted normal working. It was an unhappy period [the early 1970s]. Too many changes were coming too fast, and there were worries over manning levels.

Mars companies in the United Kingdom do not have recognised unions, so a consultative system was introduced. Each shift elected about fifteen men to a shift committee. From this, one represented them on the Pay Group (which reviewed comparable rates elsewhere as part of a pay determination procedure), one on the Procedures Group, and three on a plant-wide Review Group. The system worked well and produced gains early on. Following a claim by two unions for recognition under the 1975 Employment Act, ACAS conducted a ballot on union recognition.

The original system of consultation subsequently faded away, and was scrapped about eighteen months ago. The Pay and Procedures Groups both remain, but no new elections have been held for them. The principle of election is itself in doubt, but one of the left-over members of the Pay Group suggested that there were advantages in having continuity of membership, and he would not like to see a 'them and us' atmosphere develop.

Part of the cause of the apathy which developed towards the system was that some expected too much from it. The shopfloor saw their representatives as shop stewards. They wanted a sort of company union, but it was never intended to act like that. When it was working, some of the best people on the consultative committee were those who had wanted union recognition.

Although the consultative system has gone, it was reported that the company has not gone back to being autocratic; they get feedback from people and do not present them with a *fait accompli*. There is warning well in advance if a project is likely to involve job transfers or redundancy. A variety of working parties were set up in advance of the new canning lines being introduced. 'If they could find a way of canning meetings, the company would make another fortune.'

These respondents regarded the company as the best firm to work for in the area – it looks after you and is top of the pay league. The success of the company they ascribed to having a good product; good luck; aggressive people at the top who go in for forward planning and beating the opposition – 'You don't just sit back and wait for things to happen, you make things

93

happen round here'; always getting or evolving the right people in the right place at the right time; absence of demarcation disputes; and 'a big thing in this company', all grades being on first name terms.

COMMUNITY RELATIONS

I hope they will eventually come to see parity between them out there and us in here – even if it takes years.

(Community Relations Manager)

As well as seeking a happy, loyal and productive workforce inside the factory, Pedigree Petfoods does its utmost to be seen as 'a good neighbour' to Melton Mowbray. The relationship between the company and the town is highlighted because Petfoods is the major employer, and because the main plant is close to the centre of the town. Local external relations are the full-time responsibility of a Community Relations manager, though many other managers are involved in the company's efforts, to greater or lesser degrees. The community relations manager, according to a colleague, is 'the custodian of the relationship . . . he keeps the town sweet'. In fact he has *always* been highly active in local community affairs, but it was only in the early 1970s that the company took advantage of the fact: 'The plant was growing and becoming an economic force in the community, and there was a growth in outside issues – it was the managing director of this company who decided my role.' His activities have, however, tended to reflect his own interests. His extensive involvement extends from Rotary to the local Youth Club Management Committee, from the Manpower

Services Commission Youth Committee to the Melton Polish Club. In the town he is often affectionately referred to as 'Mr Petfoods'. Recently, however, other managers have become involved locally. As the community relations manager himself pointed out: 'I once sat on twenty-nine local committees, and later got colleagues to go in my place as a company policy.'

The community relations manager now oversees the activities of 'thirty to forty' Petfoods managers who are also involved, though to lesser degrees, in local community affairs. In this way Petfoods monitors the feelings of the local populace towards the company, and can respond accordingly by controlling lorry movements, controlling any smell and noise from the factory, making sure that the visual impact of new plant causes as little upset as possible, etc. The community relations manager himself likes to see this as 'ploughing back the profits' and ensuring company activities are 'mutually beneficial' in line with corporate philosophy, and certainly Petfoods' effort is substantial. The community relations budget itself is a sum approaching six figures, and the less tangible costs of redirecting lorry movements, shutting down production temporarily when noise or smell is excessive, building unobtrusive plant, etc., must all add up significantly. However, he insists that the long-term benefits of a good relationship with the local authority, and being known as a good employer, can only go to increase the legitimacy, and ultimately the profitability, of the company.

Until the late 1960s, this long-serving manager's role at the Melton plant was production management. Then, his local involved, though to lesser degrees, in local community affairs. he likes his company as well as the town, and today sees a 'mutual benefit' for town and company. He feels privileged in being given this full-time role. He thus took pride in one of the company's latest charitable donations – boxes of books for all the primary schools in Melton:

We made a little occasion of it and had the opportunity to talk to them – the teachers. My big hope is that the kids will get lots of chances to read lots of books that they would never have done before. I got the most glowing letters back from the teachers.

However, he will soon reach retirement age, and it seems likely that he may be replaced by a committee of professional managers. About four or five managers from various departments of Petfoods are already meeting regularly to weigh up and anticipate local authority policy, local community attitudes and pressure-group demands. Most recently, some dissent in the town over lorry movements has been voiced by People Against Lorries (PAL), and though not in direct response to this group, the committee recently has been considering switching some traffic to rail. This group will become responsible for managing Petfoods' social environment.

BUILDING BRIDGES

A recent involvement with the local community which itself carries a full-time manager is the Melton Industrial Development Award Scheme (MIDAS). This project, run in conjunction with the local council, is designed to attract labour-intensive small companies to Melton Mowbray by offering cash prizes, tax-free loans, subsidised factory premises, and free management consultation to award winners.[2] The avowed aim is to enhance employment prospects in the area, though Petfoods managers do admit that the effect so far has been small. A press release described the company's thinking behind MIDAS:

The belief that a business cannot flourish or progress in isolation from the community in which it exists is fast gaining wide acceptance. The community comprises people and people are in turn our customers, suppliers and associates. Our active help and support in creating a healthy and prosperous environment therefore is a basic obligation we cannot afford to ignore. Investment in the community is not only good sense and good citizenship but also a sound investment in our own future.

The MIDAS manager sees the scheme in these terms, and made special reference to the need to cope with the labour-displacement effects of new technology, including that of his own company:

Big companies have to invest in new technology and although Petfoods has a no redundancy policy there is bound to be a long-run decline in numbers. . . . We can't therefore provide employment for our own employees' children . . . where the hell are they going to work in Melton?

He sees MIDAS as having 'an altruistic, ulterior motive'.

Other managers who supported the MIDAS idea emphasise the benefits to the company. They said there was an 'associate relations aspect', in that Petfoods workers could be 'proud' that their company was making an effort to relieve unemployment. More specifically, said one manager, 'it's a bridge-building exercise' between the company and its local and national constituents. Petfoods seeks to develop a relationship of mutual benefit between the company and local and national state officials, by involving planners in Petfoods plans for the future: MIDAS is to be repeated on a larger scale this year.

Although Petfoods could have boasted about its efforts, and 'shouted from the rooftops', it has, in fact, been understated in promoting MIDAS, and presents itself as a trustee. Overall, however, the personnel director is pleased with the results of the company's investment in community affairs, including MIDAS: 'The newspapers have been very helpful with our community efforts, and the town council is well disposed to us. At the county council we have very constructive relationships.'

SELLING MORE BOXES

Pedigree Petfoods External Relations department engages in various public relations activities. The most important of these is concerned with the 'responsible ownership of pets'.

External relations at Petfoods is an extension of the marketing function. The reported strategy is to undertake an external relations programme which will assist the achievement of the company's short- and medium-term marketing goals, by increasing 'the levels of responsibly-owned pet animals in the United Kingdom'. Petfoods emphasises that it does not want an irresponsible expansion of the pet population. For example, an increase in the stray dog population might prompt unfavourable government intervention. One manager suggested that 'if the pet population expanded, with all the new owners being irresponsible, you could threaten a pet population collapse due to legislation'. In any case, irresponsible owners do not tend to use prepared petfood. Hence 'responsibly-owned pet animals'.

Pedigree Petfoods puts more than any other petfood company into the sponsorship of dog and cat shows. The money for this comes from Marketing, and does not affect the external relations budget. One marketing manager suggested: 'We don't sponsor, we *support*. We're putting back in small measure something of what we take out.'

Similarly, Petfoods encourages dog-training. For instance, Petfoods Breeder and Veterinary Services Manager, also chairman of the Pet Health Council, is offering a course for the training of dog-trainers, and will help in the hire of halls and advertising for dog-training classes in the cause of responsible pet ownership.

Petfoods also offers its support to, and its managers often sit on, many of the animal welfare societies. For instance, through the offices of its external relations consultants, Gwynne Hart Associates, it financially assists the Petfoods Manufacturers Association, the Pet Health Council, and the Joint Advisory Council on Pets in Society,[3] for whom the consultancy acts as secretariat. Petfoods also liaises with the RSPCA and the PDSA, since it is 'ploughing the same furrows with respect to responsible pet ownership'. A recent involvement with some of the animal welfare societies was with the 'Hearing Dogs for the Deaf' research project. Petfoods pays half, and an animal welfare society and some private sponsorship provide the rest.

The external relations manager explained that Petfoods' connection with the animal welfare societies has occasioned at least one very direct mutual benefit. Through contributions to publicity and advertising, Petfoods has helped the Cats Protection League's 're-housing kittens project'. In this case, the Whiskas brand was directly associated with the project in publicity.

A major thrust of Petfoods' external relations campaign is directed towards pet animal experts – especially breeders and vets – and one of the three external relations managers spends most of her time editing and preparing *Pedigree Digest*, a quarterly journal which aims to bridge the gap between breeders and vets. The *Digest* presents popular scientific articles of interest to both, pet animal nutrition and the benefits of pets in society being the major themes.[4] 'Readers see it', suggested one manager, 'as being a professional, unbiased,

99

authoritative and, above all, non-commercial quarterly, which reflects great credit on the company.' As well as contributions from respected breeders and veterinary surgeons, the Mars group Animal Studies Centre (ASC) scientists regularly write articles for the journal. The ASC scientists, seeing themselves as the 'conscience of the company', are keen that the original aims are maintained, and are allowed to exercise some editorial influence.

External relations wishes to uphold the scientific excellence of the ASC and to publicise this excellence among 'opinion formers' – vets, breeders, politicians, etc. The ASC was created in the first place to test the nutritional and palatability aspects of Petfoods products, as well as bringing under one organisation various pieces of applied research within the company. It has now developed into *the* expert centre on pet animal nutrition in Europe. It has forty-two 'associates', including twelve graduate scientists, many with PhDs. They are veterinarians, biochemists, nutritionists, etc.

One way of demonstrating this scientific excellence is via *Pedigree Digest*. Another is by encouraging people to visit the ASC. All final-year veterinary students in Britain, for instance, make a visit. A third means is the prestigious Annual Waltham Symposium, which attracts top animal scientists from across Europe, as well as the specialist press.

Satisfied that his research team is allowed to 'push back the frontiers' for pet animal nutrition, a senior Animal Studies Centre scientist also recognises that 'the primary responsibility of the firm is to make profits'.

Petfoods tries to reach the general public as well, with its Education Programme – an extensive service run by a full-time manager. It was explained to us that pet ownership begins very early, and that pets form a very popular topic for primary school children's projects (second only to festivals – Christmas, Easter, etc.). Teachers thus welcome free teaching materials on the subject, she says, and she distributes them via teaching centres. 'This is very useful for them because they're very hard pressed for cash.' She provides teachers with leaflets, posters, 'teaching packs', etc., and occasionally videos and 16mm films, most aimed at teaching children how to look after their pets. In some cases there are small charges. (Many posters and leaflets are also sent for use in the waiting rooms of veterinary practices.) Says a manager, 'It gets kids thinking dog or cat.' 'I see the possibilities as endless', and a print budget approaching six figures is now insufficient to meet the created demand. The Education/Advisory Research Officer said, 'I used to be a teacher, so I know that they want', and, on content, the advice is used of a respected educationalist. Brand names of Petfoods products (Chum, Whiskas, etc.) appear on many leaflets and posters, though often not in prominent positions. 'I'm sensitive to the commercial ethics question very much', she told us, and although advertising managers for the various brands produce many of the leaflets themselves, she says 'they don't force us to put them in the education packs'. She went on: 'The important thing is that they see we *care* about pet care . . . it's the future of the business.'

The education programme, together with other external relations activities, is recognised as successful in an internal document: 'There is evidence that this programme has been successful, since the numbers of cats and dogs continues to grow, despite the country's economic problems. . . . The work of our schools programme has increased, and is widely acknowledged.'

External relations has also instigated a 'Kerb Your Dog Scheme', which has now been taken up by 114 local authorities across the United Kingdom. This involves educating the public and the authorities on the stray dog problem, and on the problem of dog-fouling in public places such as parks.

Petfoods takes the pet excrement problem very seriously, and apart from its educational efforts to make people kerb their dogs, they have given one animal scientist – a PhD-qualified animal behaviourist – the task of looking for long-term solutions. The scientist concerned explained:

> Dog-fouling is a big problem . . . probably one of the bigger long-term restrictions on animals or dogs in city areas . . . so I've been doing a fair level of research on various aspects of that . . . things like faeces breakdown, choice of defecation site and looking at the effectiveness of campaigns like 'Kerb Your Dog' . . . I've also done some work with Toulouse City Council in France and with Stockholm Council in Sweden . . . and I'm also looking at the scoops – poop scoops . . . We're also doing some research into other ways of managing the problem like puppy training . . . and doing some work on attractiveness to see whether you can change the faeces site, whether there are visual cues at all.

It was hoped that chemical attractants and repellants would achieve good results, but so far they have not, and the company to date has had to rely on encouraging restraint and responsibility on the part of pet owners.

Finally, Petfoods' interests extend to the 'human/companion animal bond'. The 'negatives' about pet animals (zoonoses,[5] dog-fouling, use of scarce proteins, etc.) say Petfoods managers, have all been quantified. 'The measurable negatives,' said a senior ASC scientist, 'you can measure in grams or litres or court cases.' Petfoods would like scientifically to quantify the benefits, which are largely to do with companionship. This evidence will be used to balance the negative viewpoints sometimes expressed by doctors (zoonoses), local authorities (pollution), and the mass media (Third World human resource needs), etc.

The ASC's animal behaviourist has collected what evidence

ᴉe can on the use of pets in psychotherapy, the benefits of pets
ᴉn encouraging exercise and social contacts among owners, the
ɔenefits of pets to the elderly, etc. As yet, not much evidence has
ɔeen produced, apart from that which came from a symposium
which was organised by Petfoods, in 1974.[6] Pedigree Petfoods
therefore aims 'to provide evidence in statistically reputable
terms on the benefits of pet ownership to normal people'.
Petfoods emphasises 'normal people' because, says one manager,

> PR people always look at the worst possible outcome – you'd
> have a lot of media coverage on . . . pets as props for kooky
> people, and that would distract attention from . . . the
> ordinary elderly living by themselves or families who are
> having pets to enrich their lives . . . that's the aim . . . the way
> in which the research would be used.

Pedigree Petfoods' animal behaviourist is secretary of the
Society for Companion Animal Studies (SCAS), who are very
interested in the use of pets in psychotherapy. Pet
psychotherapy, he says, is the main area where Petfoods' and
SCAS's interests diverge:

> some of the areas of research that SCAS is involved with
> could be seen as a lower priority by Petfoods, and the best
> example is the role of pets in therapy for the elderly and
> mentally handicapped . . . Pedigree would view that as being
> fine, happy for people to look at this, but we don't really want
> the image of pets as props, as sort of crutches for the elderly
> and disabled as being seen as the main reason for having
> pets.

Petfoods envisages spending, in the near future, sums on
contracted research on the benefits of pets, and it is currently

discussing proposals with university researchers in social work, social psychology, psychiatry, etc. The high priority given to the research by Petfoods is evidenced not only in terms of the money involved, but also the seniority of the managers who have conceived of the project and are implementing it. One of them explained: 'All we're saying is that we ought to know. We take the risk that the negatives may outweigh the benefits', although 'we have an input in every stage of research design' and 'it can be counter-productive if you just hand out money.'

ENSURING CONTINUITY OF SUPPLY

As we have seen in the case of MIDAS, community relations management, responsible pet ownership and in the introduction of new technology, Pedigree Petfoods is exceptional in the way it defines responsible behaviour and incorporates that definition within corporate business objectives: fundamentally, 'running a profitable business'.

This integration of ethics – as defined by the company managers and owners – within capitalist priorities is nowhere more immediately expressed than in Petfoods' relations with its suppliers. It is a 'responsibility' area that has been widely stressed to us by our respondents.

The difficulties that the recession poses for Petfoods' suppliers intensifies matters: 'Do we cut them out because of the recession?' asked the personnel director. 'That responsibility is up against you all the time.'

In the introduction we stated that Pedigree Petfoods' ROTA principle (Return on Total Assets) dictates that the company concentrates capital expenditure on the manufacture of petfood. It seeks to contract out as many other functions as possible, but it would be misleading to suggest that it leaves their *management* to these contractors. On the contrary, Petfoods is deeply, if indirectly, involved in the management of its suppliers' businesses.

The process begins at the selection of tendering suppliers. The transport manager explained:

> We're good at manufacturing and marketing so we leave distribution to others – getting other people to put in the money and run it for us. It is very difficult for us not to run their show . . . we do investigate contractors in great detail, including their management structure and strength. We look for managers with their own ideas . . . independence of thought and creativity.

The purchasing manager listed as desirable 'continuity of supply', innovating suppliers, good industrial relations, product scheduling and financial status, flexible supply and ability to meet delivery dates, etc. Petfoods ensures these criteria are met by insisting on senior management representation on the part of its suppliers.

A large proportion of the commercial division's work is devoted to investigating suppliers to test their suitability. One manager joked: 'A lot of the work of this division is investigating . . . sorting out our suppliers. . . . Many of our suppliers think we know more about them than they do!' While another stressed 'this idea of knowing the company you're doing business with in detail'. They even investigate their suppliers' suppliers.

Being responsible towards suppliers was 'because of its long-term benefit to the company', but also because this stance was in the suppliers' best interests. For instance, on price:

> We are looking for continuity of supply at a reasonable price

. . . we pitch the balance. We do not like buying below cost, for example. . . . We will not drive prices down of our own volition.

Another manager added:

It's a long term relationship with the supplier – sometimes we're negotiating a price that will keep the weak in business. In some cases we've actually asked them to put up the prices! . . . We have had suppliers ask us for help, and we've stuck an accountant in and it's worked. It gives us a very strong position.

In addition to mutually determining prices, Petfoods gives long periods of notice and gradual run-downs of contracts it wishes to terminate, where the supplier cannot conform to its criteria; five years, in one case, for a supplier who refused to innovate. A manager enlarged on this point:

If you deal with suppliers for a long time, then there are contacts at all levels of the company. Some say we're too hard a taskmaster – that means they're not prepared to put in the effort we require; some can't stand the pace. . . . The coherent message that goes through is that we're not doing it because we're philanthropists. We do it because it's the best way of doing business: Benefits Shared Among Contributors.

He explained that Petfoods 'incents' planners within other companies to join in the drive towards 'increased consumer value-for-money'. The purchasing manager said that their message to suppliers and *their* suppliers was not to push their inefficiencies on to Petfoods: get your own house in order. That is really a mutuality of benefits, he pointed out – growing together. Just like Marks and Spencer and their supplier relations, he said.

While they would agree to place contracts for some period into the future in those cases where a supplier was making a capital investment calculated to be in keeping with Petfoods' interest, Pedigree Petfoods will not usually wholly underwrite a supplier's capital programme. The company is seeking, here, not only to avoid spending on assets peripheral to production, but also to encourage its (given) new supplier to seek other partners in trade to help increase *its* return on assets. In such a way, Petfoods can enjoy supply by a well-capitalised contractor at lower prices than would hold if Petfoods were the supplier's sole customer.

Managers emphasise that Petfoods is scrupulous about gifts and inducements – anybody offering or accepting such would be dropped.

The extent and coherence of the mutuality of benefits view at Petfoods, and its practical application, is surely exceptional, not least because it is so carefully and successfully nurtured from the top. The mutuality of benefits principle – which should sound strange to British managers – is presented to legitimise all action. The corporation continues to update the house philosophy to make sure that managers continue to use it – witness the recent world management attitude survey. In the case of supplier relations, Petfoods has managed to reconcile the conflict implicit in any business bargaining.

ATTRACTING AND RETAINING ABOVE-AVERAGE MANAGERS

The supreme business competence of Petfoods managers is witnessed in their dealings with suppliers – relatively junior managers in shirt-sleeves can successfully negotiate with directors of other companies. Their consummate negotiating skills are also deployed day-to-day within the company.

It is a conscious policy of the Mars Corporation 'to attract high calibre individuals' into its management, and it is obvious even to the casual observer that they have succeeded. Petfoods managers exude confidence and competence. Espousing a mutuality of benefits to all the company's constituents – consumers, suppliers, local and national government, etc. – helps to 'attract and retain above-average managers'. They are satisfied that mutuality of benefits would be no part of a 'back-street operation'. Many managers jokingly expressed reservations about 'being in dogfood', but clearly take pride in the fact that Pedigree Petfoods is quite distinct from the average food manufacturer.

In the last ten or fifteen years, these high-calibre managers have employed mutuality of benefits in devising their campaigns to manage their environment – their market, their workforce, the local community, etc. The indications are that this sphere is still being actively extended.

7 Summary and Political Analysis of Case Studies

This chapter draws together the basic themes and issues reported in our case studies, and provides a comparative political analysis of the differences between the firms. The first section provides short summaries of each firm, issue by issue, in order to stress the key points as we see them. This is followed by a demonstration of the limits of the contingency approach – the orthodoxy in organisation theory. We do this by attempting to marry the 'contingent variables' offered by organisation theory to company behaviours in our case studies. This will lead to a justification for a more 'anthropological' approach to corporate life. The third section of the chapter then provides a comparative political analysis of the derivation of social policy issues.

SUMMARY OF CASE STUDIES

Harveys

The important point about 'the successful integration of foreign labour' at Harveys was that there was no clear management policy on the management of the black labour force. Managers did not perceive there to be a problem. This was, no doubt, partly because there had so far been no pressure from the CRE, nor from black workers themselves or their union. (The union was not black-conscious currently, having only four black shop stewards.)

Blacks were not to be found in supervisory positions, because of a change of promotion procedures during the 1960s. There was a suspicion of the original motivation for this change, though today the new procedures were institutionalised and related by managers to mechanisation and the need for college-trained technical skills. This situation was compounded by the fact that, since the 1960s, there had in any case been few openings.

The small new school of managers, which one might expect to be more amenable to recent changes in attitude towards ethnic minorities, were as yet not in a position to make an impact on employment practices, old traditions still being entrenched.

Parker's

The new school at Parker's were becoming more dominant, with a 'softer' approach to all employment practices. With pressures from the CRE and from the black-conscious union, an enlightened response was being developed in terms of industrial language training and an assessment system. Even here, however, old school production managers were still well entrenched, and had so far resisted the implementation of the social policies of the personnel department.

On new technology, we saw a similar transition in process from a hard to a soft approach to work organisation, and on all issues the new school wished to eliminate the *confrontational* approach to the union. Here, too, a 'long, long haul' lies ahead.

On external relations there was no developed local civic–business élite for Parker's managers to join, even if they had wished to. They treated the outside world 'like the weather'.

Davis's

At Davis's, we have seen a *withdrawal* from the previous paternalistic relationship with the local community. This was partly because of outside pressures – especially the local Labour party, and also unionisation – and partly because Davis's managers had, in any case, been relieved of paternal obligations with the development of the welfare state. The new school of managers at Davis's were 'professionals', mainly from working-class backgrounds, whose values were in line with the withdrawal, and although some did have affiliations with local and national institutions, these were in a *personal* capacity. That is, their affiliations were not to do with *corporate* social policy.

On environmental pollution, Davis's had a formalised environmental plan, the bulk of which attended to the implementation of state legalisation.

Pedigree Petfoods

Pedigree Petfoods' all-embracing mutuality of benefits philosophy came from the Mars family, and had been internalised and developed by managers in the interests of furthering their careers. All the public aspects of their business were managed, their policies extending far beyond anything we saw at the other companies.

Justifications for their social policies on both external and internal issues were all in terms of instrumental business interests, though at every point these underlying rational motivations were linked to a legitimising ideology of mutual beneficence.

Some social policies – for instance, the implementation of the consultation system – were developed in response to direct pressures and 'threats', though in all cases management attempted to, and largely succeeded in, maintaining control of the political agenda by applying a thorough and comprehensive *anticipatory* rationale.

THE LIMITS OF THE CONTINGENCY APPROACH

The striking differences between our four companies lead to some of the most fundamental conclusions from our work. How do we initially explain these differences? The orthodoxy in organisational theory would point towards 'contingent variables' from which organisational design and functioning are supposed to follow. There are a host of criticisms against this over-simplified view.[1] Here, we discuss the contrasts between the firms and show why a contingency approach is inadequate.

Typical variables put across by organisational theorists include size of firm, technology, product, location and milieux, market share, the 'values variable'(!), degree of local ownership, etc. These contingent variables are supposed to systemically determine an organisation's 'response' to its environment. Following the logic of this theory, we would expect only minor differences between, for instance, Parker's and Petfoods – for they are similar in terms of size (both employ around 2000), technology (modern industrial food-processing), market share (Petfoods already has a 60 per cent share; Parker's is approaching this position quickly), and ownership (both companies are US-owned). The 'contingent' *differences* between the two companies relate to (i) geographical location and (ii) the product. Parker's is a large enterprise in a south-west Midlands city with a diverse economy, and makes products which are not generally considered contentious. Petfoods is a large enterprise in a small shire town, sharing a rural labour market and producing a commodity for a contentious population (dog owners). These are significant but not all-explaining differences.

Contingent Similarities

Of the four companies studied, Petfoods and Parker's are the most suitable for comparison. For this reason they provide the fairest test for the orthodoxy. Even on close scrutiny, contingent similiarities are very strong as regards the issues of the introduction of new technology, supplier relations and environmental pollution. If a contingency approach carried any weight, one would expect similar 'environmental responses'. However, the management of these three issues in the two companies contrasted starkly.

On technical change, despite similar basic food-processing technologies, and despite similar developments in production techniques over the past few years, the ways in which Parker's and Petfoods have dealt with the social issues raised are quite distinct. Whilst Parker's still had a confrontational approach to work organisation, for instance on manning levels and on productivity agreements (witness the warehouse saga), Petfoods had from the beginning 'consulted' with the workforce and used the latest job design techniques. Similarly, on technically-induced redundancies, whilst Parker's simply laid people off within the limits imposed by a strong trade union,

113

Petfoods developed a Manpower Reduction Programme well in advance, and made it clear to the workforce that those remaining would be upgraded with higher wages and more satisfying jobs. Further, it more recently involved itself heavily in MIDAS, the local small-business initiative scheme which, managers said, had a strong 'associate relations' aspect in that Petfoods' workers would know they were working for a company which cared about unemployment.

On environmental pollution, both firms have a comparable effluent problem and have to deal with the same water authority. Petfoods has successfully managed its own problem. It has a close and convivial relationship with the water authority and can claim to return water to the river in a better condition than when it was extracted. At Parker's, in contrast, its own efforts to treat its effluent failed years ago. Its relationship with the water authority is soured, and today Parker's managers explain their actions on this issue by reference to direct pressures from the authority. They simply comply with demands for information and for the finances for treatment.

On supplier relations, there are striking similarities between the two companies' supplier markets. That is, both enjoy a competitive supply of product ingredients while facing an oligopolistic supply of packaging materials. Yet they have completely different approaches to their suppliers. As we saw, Petfoods *manages* its suppliers, to 'mutual benefit', not being afraid to instruct a supplying firm in detail even on their internal financial and organisational affairs. Parker's, on the other hand, while admitting that there *might* be instrumental justifications for managing its suppliers more closely than it is prepared to, in practice holds itself back. This is partly on moral grounds – it wants only to be known as a good customer.

114

Contingent Differences

As far as external relations, both national and local, are concerned, there *are* contingent differences and at first sight an orthodox explanation has some success. Petfoods supplies a contentious population (dog and cat owners), and thus its managers might be *expected* to indulge in spreading the 'good news' about pet ownership. Parker's, on the other hand, has a relatively unproblematic product. Similarly, because Petfoods contrasts with Parker's in that it is a large company in a small shire town, one might expect a heavier involvement in local community affairs. Thus a developed external relations function for local and national issues at Petfoods may appear entirely logical.

However, the *extent* of Petfoods thoroughgoing management of external relations was, to say the least, beyond the bounds of duty. If anything, *causality is reversed*, with *Petfoods* defining hypothetically many of the 'pressures' it ostensibly faced from the 'external environment'. Petfoods does not simply 'respond' to pressures, but actually attempts to *manage* its environment to its own benefit. Its campaign for 'responsible pet ownership', for instance, is not simply a result of pressures from the anti-dog lobby. On the contrary, it is an active attempt to maintain and expand the responsibly owned dog and cat populations, and thus the market for its products.

Consistency

It should, by now, be clear that what is *really* striking about these two companies are their respective *consistent approaches to all issues*. Petfoods sets out to manage everything to the hilt, under the guise of its mutuality of benefits philosophy, while Parker's tends to 'treat the outside world like the weather', simply responding in an *ad hoc* manner to pressures from the trades unions, the Commission for Racial Equality, etc., as and when they arise.

The contingency approach could, of course, be saved if it could be demonstrated that one style of management was more successful in economic terms than the other, and that the firms existed in competition with others sufficient to force them to adopt one approach or face going bust. Suffice it to say here that both firms are extremely successful, having consistently increased their respective market shares over the past thirty years, and that in any case today they are both in powerful oligopolistic positions with only minor threats from competitors. Both companies are likely to be here to stay for a long time to come.

So, how do we explain the striking consistency of each company's approach to the management of various social responsibility issues? The only 'variable' which is likely for the *orthodoxy* to provide an explanation for the differences between the Parker's and Petfoods' approaches is the 'values' variable. That is, the styles, attitudes and values of the managers involved which go to make up the ethos and outlook of the organisation 'explain' the different approaches. To say the least, this begs a serious sociological question: how do values arise in practice? Only an 'anthropological' approach to organisations, which is sensitive to the day-to-day life of institutions, can come to terms with the *origins*, *meanings* and *practical applications* of values. This might disappoint those who look for an explanation in the sense presumed of the natural sciences, but we would suggest that our 'anthropological' approach is more scientific in its recognition of the human quality of action. We would also suggest that it is therefore more objective. We can illustrate the inadequacy of treating values as a variable in two ways. First, if we simply 'measure' the values of Parker's and Petfoods' managers, the result will inevitably be that Petfoods' managers are more 'humane' or 'socially-responsible', missing the vital point that there are also instrumental motives behind all these actions. For instance, responsible job design around new technology is justified on the grounds that it might avoid industrial relations unrest and create a more motivated workforce. To treat values as a variable inevitably fails to come to terms with these grounds for action. Secondly, the supposition that values are translated unproblematically into managerial practice loses sight of the complexity of the relationship between individual manager's values and those of their organisation, as well as between values and action. For instance, in all our companies some managers expressed measurable moral concern about technically-induced redundancy, yet they interpreted their responsibilities in different ways and took entirely different actions.

To understand how values, action and organisational imperatives are mediated, a more profound understanding of these matters is required than a questionnaire response could ever provide. At Parker's and at Davis's, expressed moral concerns over redundancies did not mean that managers believed it was moral, or indeed possible, to provide a private solution to the public problem of unemployment. Here, managers believed that the corporate imperative of higher labour productivity, which as managers they had to implement, caused problems of redundancy which it would have to be *other* people's business to manage. At Petfoods, on the other hand, values were *incorporated* via the mutuality of benefits philosophy, and pressed into service on behalf of the corporate imperative. Increasing labour productivity thus continued as the central objective – the 'bottom line' – while organisational members persisted in affirming the house ideology – notably through MIDAS.

Many managers did believe that although MIDAS would not provide an instant solution to the acute problem of local un-

117

employment, it was the sort of activity which was necessary. However, they justified MIDAS as much in terms of solving their own perceived private problems of industrial and local community relations as of solving the general public problem of unemployment. In any case, it has to be pointed out that MIDAS was funded largely by the state and therefore, in so far as it was successful, represented more of a *public* solution to a public problem. This leads to the general point that where companies in Britain *are* getting reinvolved in the community, their 'private solutions to public problems' are of a different meaning to the one implied by Michael Heseltine and his colleagues. This is entirely to be expected in that, even under the supposed nineteenth-century ideal, the advanced manufacturers were clear in their insistence to government that there could be only collective and therefore public solutions to massive social problems.[2]

COMPARATIVE POLITICAL ANALYSIS

This section takes four major 'social responsibility' issues, so that we may compare and contrast our companies' treatment of each, and provide explanations of similarities and differences in terms of intra-organisational processes and the politics of the issues.

Employment of Black Labour

Harveys' managers claimed to have been privately successful in 'integrating foreign labour'. This refers to shopfloor camaraderie and the absence of overt racial conflict. As we saw, this achievement has been arrived at largely spontaneously, and there was for management, therefore, 'no need for a policy'. An old school of managers who had instituted new criteria for promotion to foremanship during the early days of the recruitment of black labour no longer recognised their promotion system as discriminatory, but instead as based on the need for technical skills. Parker's managers, on the other hand, had been increasingly censured during the 1970s by a new black-conscious trade union, and indirectly by the Commission for Racial Equality. These 'external' political pressures had so far had only limited success, though personnel managers' consciousness of black issues was an outstanding feature of the company. Then new schoolers in the personnel department, however, had to face an old school of managers on the shopfloor, who had so far kept control of decisions on promotions to supervisory grades. Thus, today's stumbling block to an equal-opportunity policy lay in Parker's organisational politics. Torrington and his colleagues have emphasised the importance of gaining the commitment of *all* managers in the workplace:

> In the area of race relations changes in employment practice have to be made by many people and made effective by many more. . . . The effective translation of policy into practice does not occur unless there is a generalised commitment to that policy and the measures needed to make it work.[3]

Parker's personnel managers realise this and recognise that they have a long way to go.

To summarise, both managements, left to their own devices, left discrimination intact. The solutions to the problems facing black workers, in so far as they have been successful, have been the result of public pressure-group activity. Managers at

Parker's are beginning to respond to these pressures, and some have been 'socialised' into accepting for themselves, and advocating for others, new approaches to management practices. The problem now is to instil the new practices where it counts – at the point of implementation.

Introduction of New Technology

Three of our four firms were introducing, or had recently introduced, new machinery and production processes. In Parker's and Petfoods, we were able to examine the associated changing management of work organisation – that is, changing patterns of control and supervision of the workforce. In all three companies, we saw how managers dealt with the social problems of redundancy associated with labour-saving machinery.

Taking work organisation first, Parker's was characteristically forced to adopt a new approach to motivating and supervising the workforce in the face of a powerful trade union, and the outcome was again dependent on a battle for ascendancy between old and new schools of management. At Pedigree Petfoods, in contrast, managers anticipated the trade union 'threat', and successfully kept control of the agenda. And with no internal patronage systems, open management ensured a consistent approach to work organisation. These political differences between the firms meant their strategies had little in common apart from the quest to maintain managerial control over the quality and quantity of production and to protect large investments.

At Parker's, the conflict between the new and old schools was central to understanding their approach to work organisation. The power of the old school was challenged, as we saw, by the trade union from the early 1970s, the first strike being over manning levels at a new factory. The recommendations of the Work Study department were challenged successfully again by the union shortly afterwards in the warehouse, where the productivity benefits of the introduction of new technology were taken in the form of 'spare time' by workers. With the Work Study department virtually collapsing, and the old school generally in retreat, the new school could more recently justify and attempt to implement their new 'people people' approach to work organisation. Shift systems and work groups were reorganised in an attempt to engender 'line and shift solidarity'. Production lines and shifts were now supposed to compete with each other, with the remnants of Work Study providing a range of production figures line by line, and management supervision and control was now to be more direct rather than via the union. We might expect some resistance from the union to this new system, though during our study, the old school managers and directors were still exerting sufficient control to thwart the new school ideas. As we saw, the newly appointed site manager for the latest factory represented something of a coup for the old school – he was not the 'person person' the new school needed – and although he was more recently sacked by the new production director, several managers did comment to us that the new production director himself was taking on some of the 'autocratic' manner-isms of the old school! As in the case of the introduction of new employment practices for black labour, the move towards new forms of work organisation was being held up by entrenched managerial practices. A 'long, long haul' was ahead.

At Petfoods open management meant there was never any serious problem in gaining total management commitment to the new ideas about job design which arose in the early 1970s. The new ideas were associated with appropriate forms of supervision and worker motivation for Petfoods' heavy capital investments in new computerised production machinery at

Melton Mowbray and Peterborough in the mid-1970s. The consultation system, which has been set up around 1973 as an attempt to remain independent from unions at the time, was used to gain the commitment of workers to a system of semi-autonomous work groups. Consultation was deemed largely successful. Management authority and control was maintained, increased worker motivation and flexibility meant the full productivity benefits of the new technology were realised, and the Manning Reduction Programme associated with labour-saving machinery was accepted by a workforce with higher pay-grades and job enrichment. Managers do, however, remain worried that their schemes may in some instances have given too much autonomy to work groups, and they have introduced Zone 7 managers to head most of them.

To summarise, both companies moved towards new forms of work organisation with the introduction of new technology partly in response to trade union pressure – in the one case direct, and in the other anticipated. At Parker's, the conflict between new and old schools of management was central to understanding its approach to technology. The indications are that the new school might eventually win the battle, and it is on this success that a policy for line and shift solidarity depends. At Petfoods, it was also vital to understand its particular organisational ethos – a desire to manage every conceivable aspect to the benefit of the firm, the fear of the phantom union, and the absence of managerial politics – in order to understand its strategy. Parker's was 'social-democratic' (for want of a better term), the agenda under which new technology was set being contested both by the workforce and within management. Petfoods' approach was dominated by its single unitary ideology, which did not recognise a distinction between business objectives and worker interests – work humanisation meant increased productivity. As on many issues, the differences of interest which are actively denied by the principles of mutuality of benefits are accepted as part of everyday life at Parker's.

On technically induced redundancies, and redundancy management in general, Harveys had least in the way of a social policy. This was a legacy from pre-war employment practices. The new personnel manager was bringing new ideas about a range of employment issues, but so far redundancy management had not been in his hands, and he complained that his older colleagues' approach was simply: 'Right, two hundred redundancies, here we go!' The only refinement in the approach was a 'last in, first out' rule, which had been introduced at the union's insistence. At Davis's, managers and directors were more likely to tread softly, and as at Parker's, temporary (non-unionised) labour would take the brunt of changing market fortunes or of labour-saving machinery. The new school at Parker's complained that the old school still wished to use their 'high-handed' approach in this regard, but today could do so only with respect to temporary workers. At Pedigree Petfoods, managers went much further and, sensing possible disquiet among the workforce and the local community, they had 'involved' themselves in MIDAS, the local small-business venture aimed to attract employment to Melton Mowbray. In contrast to the other three companies, this was a *pro-active* move, in anticipation of, rather than in reaction to, external political pressures.

Local External Relations

Excepting managers' *non-corporate* involvements, and excepting the token contribution to the local-business venture, Parker's was not involved in local external relations, and never was. It 'treats the outside world like the weather', having developed during the post-war period, and therefore accepting the state's responsibility for 'the other side'. Davis's, in contrast, was originally heavily implicated in the community. However, since at least the 1930s, it had increasingly withdrawn from community relations as a deliberate act. As managers emphasised, this was in the face of a welfare state which took increasing responsibility for education, welfare, health services, etc. The new Davis's directors, most of whom had been introduced after the multinational takeover, had values in line with this withdrawal. Their working-class backgrounds, and often identification with some of the aspirations of the labour movement, meant they felt uncomfortable in being seen as paternalist, and indeed found the wrong sorts of involvements repugnant.

Pedigree Petfoods contrasted with both these companies in that, since the early 1970s, it had been *increasingly* involved in local community affairs. Perhaps significantly, in contrast to Davis's local council, Melton Mowbray has a Conservative-dominated council, though we can only guess at the importance of this factor. However, Petfoods' involvement in local affairs was quite different in character to that of the old British paternalist companies, probably having more in common with American company involvements. For Petfoods, 'involvements' are more in the style of *environmental management* than of *paternalism*. Indeed, local involvements were carefully calculated to enhance the legitimacy and long-run interests of the firm. The newly formed Social Affairs Committee, which looked like replacing the old community relations manager, would be likely to sharpen the *managed* character of local relations. And their recent proposals to form a 'one per cent club' in Leicestershire would be a strong move to further the American pattern.

For the vast majority of British companies, and indeed for our three other case-study firms, the idea of 'one per cent clubs' is alien. Much of the employer obligations which remain from before the welfare state are losing their meaning. At Harveys and Davis's, for instance, the 'chicken at Christmas' has become something to be bargained over, and thus completely changed in meaning.

National External Relations

Again consistent with its approach to the 'outside world', Parker's had only limited national involvements, and these only via the Food Manufacturers Association. Changing legislation on food additives or labelling regulations, for instance, were simply complied with rather than being seen as subject to political influence by the company. At Davis's, too, even though the chairman had a range of important personal external involvements, these were rarely corporately-inspired, and indeed against head office's stated desires.

Pedigree Petfoods was also consistent in its approach to 'National ER'. As in the cases of local external relations, work organisation, etc., a thorough and comprehensive rationale was applied. Although it perceived potential threats from the whalemeat lobby, the anti-dog lobby and other 'Green' pressures, these were always anticipated rather than direct. Rather than wait for trouble, Petfoods' approach is increasingly to maintain an influence on the agenda. National constituents are seen as subject to management. Thus, 'responsible pet ownership' is not simply a response to the anti-dog lobby but an opportunity to enhance the image of pet ownership and hence the responsibly-owned pet population, which ultimately means 'selling more boxes'. 'Good news about pet ownership' also comes via a number of other avenues: Petfoods seeks to establish and extend the credibility of pet ownership among breeders, vets and pro-dog lobbies, and ultimately therefore among the general public. Petfoods would *never* make invalid claims for pet ownership – it promotes scientific research at highly reputable and prestigious research institutions, including the Mars group's own Animal Studies Centre. However, the company would not finance research into areas where 'bad news' could be expected. In any case, as it points out, the 'bad news' has already been researched and quantified in terms of grams and litres and court cases.

Managers feel they can also legitimately influence legislation at national and European levels. At the national level, via their London-based consultants, the good opinion of Petfoods among 'opinion-formers' is sought. At EEC level, the Mars group's European social affairs committee monitors and lobbies the development and passage of legislation on a range of issues in which they have an interest. And finally, at an international level, the Animal Studies Centre is looking into ways of ensuring that the enhancement of the credibility of pet ownership prevails worldwide – most recently including Japan.

8 Managers and Corporate Social Policy

Throughout our work we have endeavoured to understand the meaning and values which inform action for managers. Only a case-study approach made this possible. The insights gained are essential to the debate on the managerial phenomenon.

MANAGERS' PERCEPTIONS OF SOCIAL RESPONSIBILITIES

British managers do not normally see themselves as confronted by issues of social responsibility, but instead by a series of day-to-day problems. This can be illustrated simply by reference to managers' reactions to our description of the project aims at interviews. We had to 'apologise' to managers for *corporate social responsibility* as an imported American abstraction, and try to concretise it by reference to specific issues – for example, health and safety at work, environmental pollution and so on:

> Well, then, we're a two-year SSRC-funded project into the [smiles] *management* of corporate social responsibility . . . case

studies . . . four firms . . . food and foundry industries . . .
good comparison . . . report-backs . . . book . . . confiden-
tial. . . . [Polite but puzzled acceptance, and slow nods.]

That is, the management of issues like health and safety at
work . . . employment of coloured labour . . . pollution . . .
and a whole range more that you could tack on the back of
them. [More emphatic nodding.]

Significantly, Petfoods managers tended to appreciate the
meaning and significance of the concept more quickly than did
the managers of the other companies. Almost invariably they
started by elaborating the mutuality of benefits principles.
Despite this, in common with managers generally, issues were
mostly not perceived as immediately moral. Rather, managers
saw the business of business as making profits and the handling
of the ethical issues examined were married to this framework,
albeit in different ways in the different companies. None the
less, as we saw in the previous chapter, the *quality* and *extent* of
social policies and their management vary widely between
companies, between *functions*, and among *individual managers*. This
is because corporate social responsibility is an abstract and
diffuse concept, open to redefinition historically, as it will be in
the future. This is in contrast to the supposition of profits,
which has always been essential to business aims. It might,
therefore, be unrealistic to expect managers necessarily to
employ social responsibility as a working concept.

In the previous chapter we also concentrated on the ways in
which particular issues were handled at our companies, and
drew attention to the values, experience and interests which
inform action. In doing this, we were able to suggest the scope
for alternative definitions of social responsibility: Parker's told
us 'We're in this business to make foods'; Petfoods told us
'We're in this business to make petfood'; etc. Despite this
common affirmation of capitalist objectives, from the *differences*

128

between our companies we could deduce that the 'bottom line' can be reconciled with managerial practice in quite distinct ways.

This chapter explores the broad limits and nature of corporate social responsibility *as perceived and acted upon by managers*. The attention is therefore on what social responsibility *ex*cludes as well as what it *in*cludes. So how do managers perceive and legitimate their social policies?

Harveys

Harveys managers provided a classic instance of *including out* – of omitting from the agenda the social responsibilities associated with the employment of a black labour force. In the eyes of senior managers at the foundry, 'there's not senior management policy because to be honest . . . I don't think there's been a call for one'. Indeed, it seems that they do not perceive the lack of blacks in even the lowest management positions as a *problem*. The 'successful integration' which they *do* perceive amounts, as we saw, to a *camaraderie* on the shopfloor. The (largely spontaneous) evolution of this shopfloor solidarity, together with the fact that there is little overt racial conflict and few trade union demands related to black issues (a partial exception being unpaid leave of absence), means that it is unlikely that this 'no problems' perception will change in the foreseeable future. Why should it?

Parker's

At Parker's, in contrast, social issues to do with the employment of black labour *were* on the agenda, this being because a militant black-conscious trade union had forced managers to recognise their demands, and because the Commission for Racial Equality had exerted some pressure on the company as regards industrial language training and promotion prospects. Even though CRE pressure came only indirectly, via the local Industrial Language Training Unit, it was sufficient to concentrate managers' attention on these issues, and indeed to help raise the consciousness, at least of personnel managers, on the employment of black labour. At Parker's then, new school personnel managers had accepted the moral validity of CRE ideas, and held a genuinely enlightened perspective towards the abilities and potential of the Asian workforce: if the *good goldfish* analogy carries any meaning, it applies in this instance. However, as we also saw, old school production managers had so far retained the prerogative of promoting to supervisory grades, and the new assessment system – designed to provide promotion prospects for blacks – had not been implemented. Personnel managers were irritated by the prejudices still held among many production managers, and were assisting the ILTU in trying to raise *their* consciousness. Clearly, they had a long way to go.

New technology and work organisation had similarly come onto the agenda at Parker's because of the strength of the trade union. The old school method of confrontation had clearly failed, and new school managers, especially the new production director, made it clear that 'line and shift solidarity' was a new means of motivating the workforce and gaining easier acceptance of changes in working practices. The new production director said that his 'style' was 'listening and involving people', rather than the 'benevolent authoritarianism' of his predecessor. However, as with the issue of black labour, 'involving people' was proving difficult in the face of entrenched shopfloor management practices.

It is important to point out here that it might be misleading simply to refer either to the old or new schools of management as 'ethical' or 'responsible' and the other as unethical, for clearly there are diverging understandings of what corporate social responsibility entails. The new school will quickly point out that the 'benevolence' of the old school goes hand in hand with a ruthless authoritarianism, stories abounding about the arbitrary harshness of their style. To distinguish their own approach, they refer to themselves as 'people people'. Equally, the old school see their own approach as based on firm but fair management, and on *loyalty* and *respect*. They modelled themselves on Harry Parker, the old family owner, who could 'hit the roof if anything went wrong, but if you were ill then he'd be the first to come knocking at your door'. The old school report that the 'democratic' aura of the new school's 'consultative' style only conceals their careerism and instrumentality – they are not 'Parker's men' at heart. Of course, what has happened at Parker's is that the old school's 'high-handed' approach is no longer accepted by the militant black trade union. Together with the changes demanded by the new US owners, this means that the old ethics of management are slowly giving way to the new, albeit by the means of a 'long, long haul' in the eyes of the new school.

Returning to specific issues, as far as supplier relations and local and national external relations are concerned, neither old nor new schools at Parker's saw much in the way of company responsibilities. Managers were keen to maintain the high quality of their products, and to keep their reputation of being a good company to supply, but never saw their responsibilities – or interests – as extending beyond these bounds. They simply 'got on with their business'. Many managers did have local connections; for instance, one personnel manager was heavily involved in the local Young Enterprise Scheme, the training manager was involved with youth clubs, and several directors sat on various local committees and charities. All these involvements, however, were in a *personal* capacity. *Corporate* involvement in local issues amounted only to token payments to a local small-business scheme, and to allowing the personnel manager permission to extend his lunch-break occasionally during attendance of Young Enterprise committee meetings. At national level, the company was involved only via the Food Manufacturers Association.

Davis's

At Davis's, in contrast to Parker's, managers saw 'treating the outside world like the weather' as a *deliberate moral choice*. One director, for instance, said, 'There are lots of things about community participation which I hate'. Almost all present senior managers and directors arrived after the company's massive withdrawal from its dominating position in local civic and political life, and their concern that Davis's should keep out in future was informed by values they learned not from the old family, but from their working-class backgrounds and experience as modern managers. As we saw, the row with the local council and pressure from the trade union forced the withdrawal. The new managers and directors are likely to ensure that it stays this way. They know that the old involvements of the past would today be branded as 'paternalism', a term carrying derogatory connotations locally.

This does not mean that Davis's managers are callous or amoral with regard to the local community. As at Parker's, there are many instances of personal *non-corporate* involvements. Rather, Davis's managers and directors feel that the old paternalism would today not be tolerated by working men and women, and that involvement in local politics would inevitably imply corruption. Certain social problems, they believe, have no legitimate private (corporate) solutions. Further, managers and directors at both companies feel they are in no position to solve certain social problems. It is not just that they feel corporate social and political activity is immoral – they simply cannot afford it. Thus when managers say that 'it's other people's responsibility' to look after the technically-induced unemployment, it does not necessarily imply a lack of concern. Indeed, at least one Davis's director felt that he was himself an employee, controlled 'with a big "C"'' by the parent company, and justified redundancies in terms of ensuring that the company remained profitable and provided at least some employment for the local community in years to come.

Pedigree Petfoods

Pedigree Petfoods management stands out as exceptional compared with our other companies for two reasons. First, their mutuality of benefits house philosophy, which all managers espouse, *does* imply *private solutions to public problems*. And secondly, whereas most of the social policies engaged in by our other companies can only be understood as responses to specific pressures and demands from various groups (the CRE, trade unions, local and national government, etc.), Petfoods' social policies are often *internally conceived and inspired in the absence of real external threats*. At Petfoods, external issues are categorically *not* treated 'like the weather': local authorities, the anti-dog lobby, changes in the law, etc., are all treated as within the compass of management. Likewise on internal pressures, for instance the 'threat' of unionisation. Managers are 'never caught with their pants down in this business'.

Petfoods managers share a unifying, authoritative ideology which is promoted in Mars managers worldwide. This ideology has been utilised by various managers in careers concerned with successfully managing these issues. It is important to note that the house ideology did not simply impose itself on these

133

managers – rather, many played an active part in defining the guidelines derived from the ideology. Through the open management system, as we saw, various managers have been able to justify – and in some cases make careers out of – the extension of various social policies, all of which have to have a demonstrable 'mutual benefit'. Thus, to mention a few, the external relations manager could justify a massive extension of national external involvements in the early 1970s, the personnel director could instigate a recent major involvement in MIDAS and other community relations activities, and the manufacturing director could engage managers in job design programmes in the mid-1970s.

A vital question is, why did Petfoods put so much time, effort and money into its social policies? To the 'outside world', managers present Petfoods as a morally concerned and ethically responsible company: job design is increasing work satisfaction; the external relations department promotes the responsible ownership of pets; local community relations activities serve to put something back into the town; MIDAS is an attempt to attract employment to Melton, etc. Inside the company, the other side of the mutuality of benefits equation is paramount. Among themselves, managers describe social policies in terms of management pay-offs – job design is increasing worker motivation and company identification, external relations is about expanding the market, and MIDAS has an 'altruistic ulterior motive', demonstrating to workers and the local community that technically-induced job losses do not mean that the company does not care about unemployment. Petfoods managers, then, do not express a primary interest in social responsibilities, but in managing every aspect of the business environment. On every issue, what can be interpreted as affective, value-laden activities also have instrumental rationales. Mutuality of benefits is corporate morality, systematically managed.

MOTIVATIONS FOR SOCIAL POLICIES

Including Out

We can now summarise the motivations underpinning corporate social policies at our four case-study companies. First, however, it is important to point out the *limits* on private solutions to public problems as perceived and expressed by managers. The majority of managers at each of our companies would consider themselves ethically responsible in their business practices, but only in Pedigree Petfoods is there any routinised code of conduct. Although this means that in some respects the other companies are 'behind' Petfoods, it also means that they are comparatively free from the contradictions implicit in all issues at Petfoods. We might characterise these managers as being concerned centrally with day-to-day management, and seeing most of the social costs of production as unfortunate but unavoidable, if they perceive the social problems at all. At Harveys, of course, senior managers did not recognise any 'problem' in the lack of blacks in supervisory positions. Their 'successful integration' (i.e. shopfloor camaraderie and a lack of overt conflict) constituted, in their eyes, a privately-achieved solution to all the questions raised by the employment of a black labour force. On many issues in Parker's and Davis's many managers *did* recognise public problems, but saw no possibility of private solutions.

Thus they saw technically-induced unemployment as an unfortunate but inevitable effect of their quest for higher productivity, yet felt that the solution had to be someone else's business, i.e. the state's. Parker's realised that their 'no redundancy' policy would not prevent unemployment, for temporary labour is omitted from the policy. And Davis's managers emphasised that the best way they could help the local employment situation was to rationalise whenever necessary in order that the company stay in business, and thus provide at least some employment in the years to come. Similarly, Parker's effluent problem was devolved to a state authority; and its external relations activities were hardly well developed, as is illustrated by its non-active involvement (via subscription) with the West Midlands Business Venture – it leaves the 'outside world' to manage itself. Ironically, *this divestment of responsibilities helps to leave individual manager's morality intact*. Thus Parker's engineering director is genuinely concerned about 'who is looking after the other side?'; personnel managers maintain a real respect for, and interest in, the culture of the Asian workforce; and some older directors are apprehensive about alienation of control over Parker's destiny and the lost community.

Managers at Davis's and Parker's recognise more readily the contradictory nature of some of their activities. They do not pretend that they are in control, and would refuse to attempt to incorporate the dilemmas they perceive within a mutuality of benefits principle. Indeed, at Davis's there has been an active withdrawal.

Response to Direct Pressures and Threats

Many social policies at Parker's and Davis's were changed, and sometimes created, in direct response to real pressures and threats from the companies' constituents – for instance, Parker's new 'people people' approach to work organisation and to the black labour force. In this case, as we saw, pressures especially from the trade union were, in fact partly responsible for the ascendency of the new school managers with a whole new approach. And at Davis's, the introduction of a set of directors with values more compatible with the changing political situation in the town could hardly have been seen as a coincidence. Similarly, the implementation of government legislation on environmental pollution caused both companies to pay for the control of their environmental impact. And at Pedigree Petfoods, the implementation of a consultation system was a direct response to the (then) immediate 'threat' of unionisation.

Responding to social pressures as and when they arise is probably typical of British companies, giving British capitalism a flavour of social democracy when compared to, for instance, Japan and America, where companies often take the initiative in developing corporate social policies. In Britain, the typical corporation is thus, in an important sense, 'constitutionalised'. Where our own companies did take the initiative – most commonly, of course, at Pedigree Petfoods – it was often justified in terms of the best way of doing business in the long run.

Commercial Rationales

Responding to social pressures can, of course, be seen as one aspect of 'the best way of doing business'. After all, if a company fails to comply with legislation or take note of trade union demands it may not stay in business at all for very long. Often, however, in the *absence* of obvious pressures, managers expressed the notion that behaving 'fairly' was the best way to ensure profitable production. Thus the supplies director at Parker's would occasionally pay for (though not necessarily use) a doubtful consignment of raw food-stuffs on the grounds that the supplier in question was likely to come up with better produce in the future. Line and shift solidarity at Parker's was similarly supposed by new school managers to make for a more flexible and more highly motivated – and thus more productive – workforce. Some managers, however, wished to qualify the notion that 'fair' deals were the most profitable, suggesting that claims by 'fair' managers that they were acting in the best long-run interests of the business were occasionally used to conceal 'cosy relationships'. (In making this comment we do not imply criticism on our part.)

At Pedigree Petfoods, where the 'fairness of profits' rationale was taken to its logical conclusion, 'cosy relationships' had been recognised as a 'problem', and where deemed unnecessary were abolished. Thus supplies managers were regularly rotated so that the commercial interests of Petfoods were always on the table in the regular negotiations with suppliers. Convivial relationships were, of course, highly desirable in some areas – for instance, local and national external relations – and here the company made use of socially competent managers with good contacts. In these cases other means of ensuring that the cosy relationships were to company benefit were used – for instance, well-defined job descriptions and management performance criteria. Hence the external relations manager's enthusiasm for his role being conceived in terms of conventional marketing criteria.

The commercial rationale for social responsibility activities is seen most clearly in the campaign for 'responsible pet ownership', whose managers were ultimately responsible to the marketing director.

Advertising and Marketing

Petfoods' national external relations activities are especially pertinent to this category, for they are all supposed ultimately to 'sell more boxes'. Appropriately, external relations is located within the marketing department and the head of external relations measures his performance against corporate market-ing criteria. Clearly the product, as with for instance drugs and babyfood, lends itself to this activity, and the massive market share of the company ensures that 'a good deal for the trade' means a good deal for the company. In contrast, the only 'responsibility' activity at the other companies which is connected to marketing is their concern with the quality of the product. And even here, they interpret their concern with quality as a simple *anticipation of a market demand* rather than, as at Petfoods, an attempt to *manage* the market. At Petfoods, external relations is an extension of the marketing function. Many readers might think this obvious, but the external relations manager assured us that external and public relations in most other United Kingdom companies are 'just for junketing'.

External Ideology

Some corporate social responsibility activities are intended to maintain and extend the preserve of private enterprise. By pointing out the 'good news' about private enterprise and initiative, the intention is to retain a belief in the virtues of competition and profits against the 'dissipating forces': the state, nationalised industries, socialism, pressure groups, etc.

Taking Parker's and the Young Enterprise Scheme, the personnel manager involved believes as much as the next man in free enterprise. However, his commitment to Young Enter-prise is more because of his concern with the transition from school to work for children, than it is for 'saving capitalism'. For Parker's, this project is not, in any case, corporately-driven. For a minority of sponsoring companies, in contrast, their involvement is both corporately-sanctioned and ideologically-inspired. This is especially the case for a local

US-controlled company, whose international personnel administrator emphasises the ideological component. He worried that 'kids these days don't know the meaning of the word profit'.

Petfoods are clearly concerned with free enterprise ideology and carry out their activities in this area through the personnel department, in consultation with the board. MIDAS is the ideal example from our case studies, which is inspired by the belief that local unemployment might be relieved through the generation of small private businesses ('little acorns grow into giant oak trees', and so on).

Internal Ideology

This category applies only to Petfoods, where most social responsibility activities receive some part of their justification by reference to managerial morale. The mutuality of benefits philosophy is central to internal ideology, and indeed was devised in the first place partly out of a concern to 'attract and retain above-average managers'. Many managers have jokingly expressed to us reservations about 'being in dogfood', and clearly draw comfort in the realisation that Pedigree Petfoods is quite distinct from the average food company. Open management, leadership in enlightened personnel and commercial practice, community consciousness, and a good external reputation, each foster this morale in various ways, and managers are frequently invited to identify their roles in terms of the house philosophy. In this way morale is actively built, and 'above-average managers' are 'attracted and retained'.

Non-corporate Social Responsibilities

Managers' rationales are not necessarily confined to the corporate objectives listed above, nor to defending the domain of private prerogatives against public encroachments. This applies more at Parker's and Davis's than at Petfoods. At Petfoods, managers' investments in the community are *demoralised* and pressed into service for the corporation. There may be a few exceptions, for instance, one animal scientist's attempt to keep his work in the Society for Companion Animal Studies independent from his identity as a 'Petfoods man'. But at the same time he recognised a mutual benefit for the company in the independence of a pressure group which upholds the benefits of pet ownership. As the animal scientist said: 'It's very important for SCAS to be independent, otherwise it folds.'

At Parker's and Davis's one is more likely to find individuals with their *own* reasons for investing in the community. A personnel manager's involvement in Young Enterprise is an ideal example. His motivations were personal ones ranging between a concern with the welfare of young adults to affirming his identity among a new generation of managers. Even his concern to defend free enterprise was not corporate-inspired, but drawn from managerial circles *outside* the corporation. Examples from many other managers in our companies included parish council work, involvement in Boy Scouts and youth clubs, the organisation of social functions for employees, talks to schools, safety lectures, and so on.

POLICY IMPLICATIONS

In conclusion it can be seen how profoundly different the social policies of private manufacturers can be. The difference extends well beyond managerial practice *per se*, for it attaches to the distinct respective ambience of the companies and touches on speech, mannerisms, styles, even the decor. The first three companies were more *plural* and less *managed*. At Petfoods, they manage to the hilt, going well beyond the conventional British wisdoms of where the boundaries of management lie. They are urgent and progressive where the other companies are more conventional and sedate.

In Chapter 1 we posed a series of questions on the nature and limits of corporate social policies which have been answered above. To conclude, we shall draw out what we consider to be the implications of our findings for managers.

Managing Public Interest

The potential dangers of managing beyond the bounds of the conventional wisdoms are considerable and diverse, and some damage to public, as well as private, interest is probable. We have experience of some companies who have had their 'fingers burnt' in the past by becoming embroiled in 'politics'. Some conflict between private and public interest is natural and inevitable, so it is risky to 'manage politics' as Petfoods seeks to do. Where there are *real conflicts of interest*, the public will tend eventually to see through any claimed 'mutuality' that is not sustainable, and beyond into the corporate purpose. It is inadvisable, therefore, to attempt to define the interests of other groups in advance on their behalf. Matters beyond the boundary should be, as the managing director of Parker's described them, 'the Imponderables'.

142

In Britain the strength of public interest groups and their real effect in changing company practices on a range of issues should not be underestimated. As we saw at Davis's and Parker's, the Commission for Racial Equality, the trades unions, and environmental pressure groups (via changing legislation), to name a few, had all been important influences on company social policies. In this sense the typical British company is already partly 'constitutionalised' – is is not just corporate-defined interests which come on the social policy agenda. On the other hand, Petfoods is more often in control of the agenda, albeit sometimes in response to perceived threats, and often with conceivably beneficial outcomes.

This is not to say that managers are not a vital group in defining corporate social responsibility, for they have choices to make on the type of response their companies will make to social pressure, and it is *they* who have to implement policies. As we saw at Parker's, these are hardly straightforward tasks, and depend on intra-organisational politics *among managers themselves*.

A Safe House for Managers?

Managers carry some responsibility for the definition of the responsibilities they assume. In order for them to be able to make an assessment independently of *corporate interests*, some *alternative bases of allegiance* are vital, and we would favour the *professionalisation* and *unionisation* of *managers*.

In the first three case studies, allegiances other than to the organisation already existed. For instance: Davis's directors frequently commented that they felt they had more in common with their workforce than with the multinational owners, and . consequently recognised the needs and aspirations of workers; old school directors at Parker's identified with the local

143

company rather than Head Office in America, and consequently were resisting the imposition of certain bureaucratic procedures; and we frequently found conflicts of interest between managers of different functions in all companies except Petfoods. It is precisely in the realisation of the 'dangers' of *professionals* to corporate interests that Pedigree Petfoods manages professional identifications through the open management system, which 'knocks the corners off' (except for the special case of the group's animal scientists in the Animal Studies Centre). At the other companies, managers can wear their professions more easily. It is because alternative bases of allegiance are antithetical to instrumental bureaucratic rationality that there is a tendency for them to be resisted when they breach the defined organisational interests. Thus *managers will have to organise themselves before they can play the independent brokerage role as 'good goldfish' that fifty years of the managerialist thesis claims they already can*. Otherwise, managers are *increasingly*, rather than decreasingly, likely to find capitalist rationales for their social policies.

Our recommendation might receive widespread support from sociologists of each of the three persuasions, Durkheimian, Weberian and Marxist. Durkheim's advice on professional societies is well known. They would save occupational groups from amorality, or 'anomie' as he termed it.[1] For Weber, bureaucracy had enormous virtues of efficiency in matching ends and means, but it always threatened all but instrumental values.[2] Professional identification might, therefore, be seen as a challenge to the bureaucratic imperative and routine. For Marx, the conflicts of interest between the corporation and the population at large were all the more severe.[3] A safe house for 'whistle-blowers' would help curtail the power of corporations, would sanction and maximise the ambivalence found among managers about 'business' in general, and would affirm their experience and perception in terms other than a *corporate career*.

Finally, our recommendation has to be seen in the light of the fact that *in none of our case studies did professions appear to be central* in defining social policies. Where they do exist, managerial unions are unsure of their direction and suffer from split instincts, *vis-à-vis* corporate and popular pressures. Industrial management is the least professionalised of all occupational groups. We would, of course, recognise certain dangers in professionalisation – for instance an overemphasis of qualifications rather than practical ability. The point here is that serious professionalisation could provide the basis for the development of an independent *social ethics of industrial management*.

New Wave?

Readers will be aware of the importance we attach to our fourth case study, Pedigree Petfoods. Certainly the most successful, and arguably the most *advanced* of our companies, Petfoods shares a great deal in common with some of the famous advanced corporations in Japan (especially on management control systems and industrial relations) and America (especially in external relations). The question is, could its extension of the boundaries of management represent a *new wave* in Britain? Certainly, as we saw in Chapter 1, there is a new mood nationally among many politicians and business leaders that the time for *private solutions to public problems* has returned, with corporations being urged to take on extra social responsibilities. There have been rumblings along the same vein also from the business schools in Britain and across Europe, with managers being urged to pay attention to the 'legitimacy threat' to the free enterprise system.[4] The evidence from our other case studies, however, which are probably more typical, would suggest a definite *no*, or at least that the *new wave* faces a

145

long, and probably bitter, struggle. At Davis's, we saw that the trend was for a withdrawal from the provision of *private* solutions, and there was little indication that managers might suddenly move in the opposite direction. And at Parker's, where on some issues one could see *new wave* ideas amongst the new school (for instance on work organisation), there was a 'long, long haul' in progress. The whole of British 'treat the outside world like the weather' management is unlikely to change overnight.

In any case, one may legitimately question the sense in which the *new wave is* providing private solutions to public problems, for in practice, as we saw, many corporate social policies have more to do with ideology or straightforward commercial rationality than the provision of real solutions. Small business venture schemes are probably a classic instance of the former, and national external relations of the latter.

The question of defining the nature of private solutions and 'social responsibility' is crucial. There are strong indications of a new confidence among government and industry that there can indeed be private solutions to public problems. On the one hand, there is Michael Heseltine's argument with which we opened this book, and that is that industrialists may re-invest both economically and morally in the community. He has in mind the great wastelands of our declining industrial cities, and refers back to the last half of the last century to *civic gospel* and economic advance by progressive owner-managers. On the other hand, within industry today there are certain corporations who again advocate private solutions. However, they do so in a rather different sense. For these companies, any social investment must have a commercial pay-off, and their managers are, unlike the nineteenth-century industrialists, much less concerned in promoting the general welfare as an end in itself. Thus Fiat's promotion of the World Wildlife Fund was really about *selling* Pandas, not protecting them. Similarly, business sponsorship of the arts and sports is always to do with public relations and free advertising. The ever-increasing number of companies involved in small-business initiative projects, à la Pilkington, help buy acceptance of massive redundancy pro-grammes. And the motivations behind the distribution of free 'educational materials', on drugs and prepared baby foods, for instance, are always suspect – witness the recent Nestlé controversy. Real solutions to the problems facing, for instance, inner-city communities like Toxteth are hardly likely to be solved by these activities. *The new wave simply does not set out to do so.*

On top of this, there are two other major problems with the idea that there are private solutions to public problems. First, British corporations rarely have the spare funds available, for instance to improve welfare, medical and education services. Secondly, from our case studies it is clear that British managers generally do not see their role as providing private solutions, nor would they wish to. A Davis's manager summed it up thus:

> New technology always aims to engineer people out. Machines are very much more predictable than people, and secondly, various things government has done to protect interests of people have militated against. For example, if we can have machinery that will work with fewer people, it's very much easier to switch it on and off according to demand. People, on the other hand, have rights – you can't pull the plug out on people.
>
> We quite clearly aim to engineer people out of our company. I believe, on a personal level, that the next big industry must be leisure. It's a national government prob-lem, *not ours.* Honestly and truly, our problem here is not to think about what to do with 3.9 million unemployed on the streets. We pay the government to look after that.

A Dilemma for Management

The reassertion of the role of *private solutions to public problems* presents an acute dilemma for industrial management. Nineteenth-century paternal welfarism included some genuine attempts at private solutions, though in the second half of the century there was increasing pressure on the state to take on the responsibilities which the owner-managers were finding a burden. With working-class pressure for the provision of public solutions coinciding with this pressure from capitalists, a modern British Social Democracy could become established, with the welfare state being finalised after the Second World War.

For managers two advantages have followed. First, they are relieved of both the direct financial and moral burden of private responsibility for housing, unemployment, education, health services, etc. Secondly, they have been able to preserve intact a capitalist ideology. With state intervention, including nationalisation, managers can blame the state for mismanagement, as if 'free enterprise' were the only means to efficiency. Hence the boardroom banter about 'lame ducks' and 'non-productive' public enterprise 'riding on the back of the private sector'.

Typically treating the outside (social and political) environment like the weather, managers can feel relieved of some personal moral dilemmas, and espouse the ideology of free enterprise while remaining, it appears to us, fundamentally committed to British social democracy and the relatively passive societal role which this implies for the firm. But if the current re-advocacy of *private solutions* is more than rhetorical, then the implicit contradictions in this situation will be highlighted. Without a coherent supporting philosophy, and with little practical guidance or experience, managers would need to become involved in new socially valuable activities.

Their personal and political moralities would be tested, the ideological target of state involvement would recede, and their tacit commitment to social democracy would be tried. In effect, another form of managerial revolution would have to take place.

Appendix: Theory and Methods of Research

At the level of grand theory, the relationship between the business enterprise and society has received the attention due to it. But in terms of empirical research it is that rare animal, a truly 'under-researched area' – a 'field in search of a focus'.[1]

The research project conducted for this book responded to this situation in two ways: first, to establish a working conceptualisation of the field, including a preliminary survey of the fundamental ideas of 'the corporation' and of 'society'; and secondly, to concentrate the empirical research on the management process where, it was argued, business–society relationships must materialise and are contested.

This can be illustrated by reference to Figure 1.

Broadly speaking, all social theories have their roots in the grand conceptions of society listed bottom right. Either functionalist – viewing society as harmonious and self-regulating; action-based – with an emphasis on the perceptions and actions of individuals and groups of actors; or class-based – which emphasises competing class interests. With a grounding in these theories, there is the literature indicated in the bottom left, which points up the nature of the modern business corporation and its roles and relationships within society. Depending on the view of corporations which is taken, different interpretations of the nature of management functions, actions

Appendix

Research Focus

	Corporation	Society

Research Orientation		Corporation	Society
Applied		Business policy Corporate strategy The management of corporate responsibility	Regulation Public policy Pressure groups
		Corporations and their constituents Legitimacy Social audit	
Theoretical		Theories of organisation and the corporation: Managerialist school Classical school Conflict school	Theories of society: Functionalist Action Class-based

FIGURE 1

SOURCE   Developed from J. E. Post, 'Research into Business and Society', AACSB Conference (Berkeley, Calif., 1981).

and interests are generated, and these have especial implications for the debate on the management of corporate social policies.

TOWARDS A RESEARCH FOCUS

There are two literatures which inform this area of interest. First, there are the alternative general theories of capitalist society, involving quite different political, economic and social analyses of the relationship between corporate and other interests. Rival consensual and conflict approaches in sociological theory must be involved in interpreting what corporations do, and they involve different views of the relationship between corporations and the state. These fundamental positions are linked, for example, with radically different views of the nature, origins, extent and limits of socially responsible business behaviour. Consensual theory, by asserting the essential compatibility of interests between the corporation and its constituencies, carries the implication that the practical limits to corporate responsibility are quite loose. Thus the 'normal' objectives of business, such as commercial success, would be seen as leaving managers considerable room for meeting the majority of demands placed on any given company. However, if one conceives of capitalist society in terms of basically antagonistic group and class interests, then the scope of managerial discretion to satisfy 'responsibility' demands would be claimed as much narrower.

An example of a theory of society based on the presumption of consensus is provided by *functionalism*. Central to this approach is the application of a biological analogy to social structure. Broadly speaking, social groups and institutions are seen as interdependent, always tending to equilibrium and stability. The conception is 'functionalist' because each of the parts is seen to function for the others. It is a system of mutual dependence. Functional systems are also readily found in economic theory, especially in the theory of price, where equilibrium is achieved through the market mechanism. The 'environment' is supposed to dictate what the firm will do; a corporation either acts in a certain way or is destroyed. This ideal has an effect in the literature on the corporation. Thus in functionalist analyses of organisations, it is often possible to sense this ideal-typical model reappearing in answer to questions of corporate social responsiveness. Corporations, it is argued, must act responsibly and *responsively* or face serious long-run difficulties of legitimation or profitability and growth. In extreme cases, firms can apparently be treated as black boxes, where the dynamics of behaviour are assumed to be an automatic or mechanical outcome of exogenous environmental changes. And in the literature on corporate social responsiblity, the heavily quantitative emphasis is premised on a positivistic approach to the measurement of social facts as determinants of corporate 'behaviour'.[2]

The majority of (mostly American) writing on corporate social responsibility clearly, if unselfconsciously, embraces these core assumptions.[3] Amongst these writers, the dominant view is that corporations are essentially responsive to social criticism and alive to the realisation that if they fail to respond to the changing consensus, then their 'future legitimacy', and even commercial success, will become problematic. But in the effort to accommodate to environmental change, the internal adjustments so necessitated must also satisfy the organisation's internal and other constituencies as far as is possible. Thus internal and external interests should reach acceptable compromise. This stress on the open society which is a feature of functionalist analysis of modern social systems has, therefore, a natural theoretical affinity with the *managerialist* view (see page 14).

An example of a theory of society predicated not on consensus but conflict is provided by what we have labelled in the previous diagram as a 'class-based' or 'radical' aproach. This questions the openness of the social system on the basis of an actual concentration of economic and, more questionably, political power, and also on the basis of a critique of managerialist theories of capitalist development of the Berle and Means type. It is argued that struggle over contradictory class interests is the secret in explaining the nature and direction of social change. Organisations would tend to be conceived of as *crystallisations* of class society, rather than as discrete entities which can be distinguished from their environments.

A company's internal and external relations would be seen as being cast within a 'contested terrain' over the priority of 'accumulation', in which is determined the nature and extent of corporate responsibility: for example, to create jobs but not to cure unemployment; to limit environmental impact 'within reason'; to create healthy working conditions, but within the limits of profitability; to enhance the quality of working life, but not to divest control into the hands of operatives. The conflicts of class interest involved in compromising profitability and health would be presented as a negation of the functionalist treatment of organisations in terms of unitary goals or human needs and, indeed, any attempt to present company policies as if they *did* represent the interests of all sections would be treated with suspicion.

It is the second theory, the *action* approach, which presents the most difficulty when it comes to locating it paradigmatically. But it is important to establish the true status of an action theory of organisation in order to be able to assess its logical implication that managers, as creative subjects, may have high discretion to determine how their firm *qua* organisation will function.

With the action approach, the focus is on a subjectivist view of the world, which argues that the social structure – in that there is one – is created in meaningful human action. As Berger and Luckmann put it, reality is socially constructed through an infinitude of individual, meaning-conferring and meaning-guided actions on a day-to-day basis: '*All* social reality is precarious; all societies are constructions in the face of chaos.'[4] The thrust of this perspective is towards rejecting the idea that there are 'systems' functions and 'organisational' goals.

If this is the essence of the action perspective, what concrete implications does it carry for the study of organisations and, more particularly, business corporations? First, the action frame of reference would seem to render the following advances.

(i) An emphasis on the problematic nature of social order

carries the implication that the power structure of the factory is capable of redefinition. This, at least, suggests the possibility of significant social change (rather than mere systemic adjustment).

(ii) Concerning managers, the focus would be on how they create 'meaningful definitions of the situation'. These definitions and their revision would relate to the way a company acted, or decided not to act, in any particular instant; they amount to the creation of 'the rules of the organisational game'. It would be of interest to an action theorist to see whether those rules were activated according to a shared set of conventional symbols, or whether they were actually being negotiated in an overtly political way.

In contrast to the orthodoxy it attacks, the action frame of reference lends itself particularly to qualitative observation of process; the question of how meaning is given, constructed and negotiated in organisations.

What does our summary of functionalist, action and class-based (radical) approaches to organisation theory tell us? Perhaps a general feature of the debate in organisation theory is the extent to which different authors fundamentally disagree as to what is the basis of organisation theory, or what it should be. And associated with these differences are different political orientations.

Secondly, there is a tendency to use the term organisation as a euphemism for the corporation. One's attitude to this must be coloured by whether one seeks a *general* theory of organisation, or whether one wishes to treat the corporation as a specific species of organisation. *Functional* and *Action* schools, as *general theories of organisation*, would not be embarrassed by the criticism that they failed to account for the special nature of the corporation. Their intention differs from the Marxist radicals, whose aim is to be 'historically specific' and who, while claiming greater precision over capitalist organisations and the

155

class nature of capitalist society, have not yet satisfactorily tackled the issue of organisations in state socialist society.

The divergencies in the literature on organisations were at least partly reproduced in the research team – one by instinct a neo-functionalist, but with a recognition of the value of the action approach; one a clear follower of Silverman's action theory; and one a radical – though he also recognised the value of the spirit behind the action frame of reference. We were, however, unanimous on the need for intensive, qualitative research into the nature of management practice. This focus is of strategic significance in the testing of the major positions in the theory both of organisations and of the corporation, so important issues are at stake: the 'neo-functionalist' in the team was interested in general organisational theory and was sympathetic to the view that, indeed, the separation of ownership from control may have enhanced the sensitivity of the corporation to a greater number of constituent interests. The expectation was of considerable managerial discretion and *de facto* power. While there has been a half a century of theorising in this area, few have attempted to make any kind of empirical exploration.

A second worker approached the issue of managerial discretion bearing Silverman's reminder that organisations are founded in human action and purposes. His past research experience suggested that there is considerable variation in the way firms negotiate (formally or informally) the introduction of new technology. What struck him was the essential 'pluralism' of such bargaining and decision-making in the West Midlands engineering industry.[5] And he, too, expected to find substantial scope for managerial discretion and 'open' corporation organisation.

The third worker was more aligned to the radical position, and believed that the changing nature of corporate ownership and control need not bring about an alteration in the logic of capitalistic enterprise and, indeed, may tend to intensify it. He expected to find that managers will use their autonomy from old styles of owner-management to free the corporation from the earlier paternal and 'affective' objectives which are now generally in decline. The definition of appropriate corporate social responsibilities would, he believed, turn on questions of long-run economic performance and political power. This more cynical view, nevertheless, required to be explored empirically, within enterprises.

These hoary old debates could not be laid to rest on the strength of a single research project, but we hoped that the discipline of empirical research and theoretical argument would offer some clarification and advance.

METHODS

Existing Empirical Work

The existing empirical work in the area of corporate responsibilities is characterised by an atheoretical approach, in that it does not discuss alternative theoretical bases for studying the topic. However, it does adopt an unselfconscious stance which might be termed positivist/functionalist. Corporations are treated as if they simply adapt to their 'environments', and writers try to relate corporate social responsibility mechanisms and responses to organisational characteristics and effectiveness with the apparent lack of appreciation of 'structural' conflicts of interest implied in their unitarist themes.

Typically, these studies consist of postal surveys requesting managers to indicate their company's involvement in a list of 'socially responsive behaviours', and rank them in order of

157

importance. Such studies yield some description, not of corporate social involvement directly, but of what companies (or at least their chief executive or his delegate) *claim* their involvement to be, on their (unstated) interpretation of the terms used in the different researchers' questionnaires. A review of this literature has been provided by Aldag and Bartol.[6]

A refreshing alternative method is employed in Ackerman's classic in this field, *The Social Challenge to Business*.[7] Ackerman, instead of relying on remote questionnaire surveys, utilises the case-study approach, taking us inside the firm to glimpse the managerial processes involved in dealing with environmental pressures. However, he shares the orthodox functionalist approach to corporations, in that he sees firms as logically adjusting to external imperatives, the role of the manager being reduced to one of the rational 'messenger'. This is reminiscent of Berle and Means' conception of managerialisation,[8] in which the manager becomes the neutral 'arbiter of the public good'. However, the discretion which Ackerman allows his managers relates only to the *timing* of responses, not to their content. Ackerman identifies no qualitative choices for management, and does not seriously treat the possibility of intra-organisational politics.

We followed Ackerman into the firm, but without his functionalist assumptions. Rather than displaying associations between organisational and environmental variables, and seeing managers as the mere facilitators of these abstract relationships, we wished to explore the exercise of the management task in relation to particular issues. This means more than augmenting Ackerman's treatment of managers as rational messengers with a recognition of 'management values' *per se*. Clearly, the notion that the ways in which corporations respond depends *simply* on the 'values' or 'ideologies' of those who run them is equally naïve. Rather, although we recognised the importance of values and ideologies, we also took into account the facts that (i) management decision-makers act within definite social contexts,[9] (ii) different relevant actors may have different values, and (iii) intra-organisational political processes are important.[10]

Given our theoretical concerns, it was appropriate to examine firms intensively – to understand the day-to-day realities of managing; and longitudinally – to illustrate the decision-making processes which, over time, determine firms' social activities.

Our Approach

We began our fieldwork with the intention of exploring three aspects of management which, when combined, would permit analysis and interpretation of business behaviour relating to social policy issues.

1. *Management Discretion*   This represents a vital element in empirical research into the dynamics of corporate responses to the social environment. The extent and limits of management discretion is of great interest, whatever the theoretical standpoint adopted. Information, from documents, conversation and observations, was gathered on the background, interests and activities of managers at all levels, to permit an analysis of the extent and limits of their discretion by reference to:
- their perceived interests, both personal and coalitional;
- inter-role conflicts arising from a manager's membership of different groups inside and outside the firm, including professional bodies, class location and generational affiliation;
- organisational targets (especially profits) and management control systems, and their impact in permitting or limiting the exercise of discretion;

– the implied 'rationality' which might serve to limit tacit agendas for organisational choice; non-decisions.

2. *Company Strategies*   Corporate behaviour in respect of 'social issues' can be represented as a strategic, if frequently unconscious, choice between an evaluation that the long-term interests of the firm would be served by active responses to anticipated changes in the social environment, or that the outside world is to be treated 'like the weather': passively. This demanded fieldwork which focused on the processes of strategy formation, both formal and informal.

3. *External Relations*   Both the formulation of strategy and the exercise of management discretion will be affected by managers' contact with, and perceptions of, the firm's environment. This merited attention as a distinct focus because all levels of management, formally or informally, are involved in external relations, broadly defined. Thus there was a focus in the fieldwork on the outside roles and relations of directors, public affairs and external relations officials, and the firm's interactions with pressure groups and various regulatory authorities. Management recruitment and training is also important, carrying implications for the organisation's perceptions of, and responses to, its environment. This raises questions over the definition of managerial ethos, differences between 'new' and 'old' schools, and over the managerial career or life-cycle.

There have been three ways of data gathering, all of which are common to intensive studies of organisation, namely interviews, sitting-in, and studying documents. This amounted to an 'anthropological' approach to the fieldwork. Out of intensive observation over an extended period, we were able to develop a thorough understanding of the *tribal* differences between the firms' managements, and of a complexity of processes that produced each firm's particular character, ideology and ethos.

Appendix

Problems of Access and Publication

Whilst discussing research methods, it is worth commenting on the problems of access we have encountered. First, it should be pointed out that the initial granting of access is not the end of the problem. Rather, access has to be continuously renegotiated. It has constantly to be borne in mind that the firm's agreement that research may be carried on into its activities may change during the course of the research, and that both the agreement of individual managers and access to specific information must be gained on frequent occasions. This was brought home to us most especially in what turned out to be an abortive case study early in our research. We found that although the firm agreed that we should be allowed to carry on research, doors were closed to us when it came to interviewing certain managers and gaining certain types of information. Then, later, the firm brought our study to an abrupt end.

The second, related problem of access concerns the initial avenue of access which is used. Our experience suggests that it is best to gain access via as high a level of management as possible – preferably the managing director of the firm – and that when studying issues towards which the workforce is sensitive, the appropriate trade union official (normally the works convener) should be approached at the outset. In two of our four companies, initial access was via the approval of the managing director, and our access to specific meetings and other sources of information has been excellent. In one of these firms, however, the shop stewards committee was not approached until later, and some resistance by the stewards to our studying certain workforce-related issues was experienced. In the other two companies access was via functional directors, and this meant we met certain constraints on the scope of our studies. In particular, as a consequence we found some difficulties in gaining the cooperation of other directors of equivalent status. This problem is not insurmountable, but again the implications are clear for initial approaches to companies when studying the higher reaches of the organisation. Where possible, go in at the top.

Of course, while being frustrating, these methodological problems told us how to carry on future research. They also told us something about the internal politics of our case-study firms, for example relating to the interests, conflicts and relative status of departments or the power of a trade union.

Because managers are not used to being themselves the objects of study, together with the intensity of contact we needed, and also the sensitive nature of the issues, problems of gaining and maintaining access were expected. In practice, it should be said, however, that all the firms, and their managers, who participated in the project were most helpful.

All these factors also have a bearing on the question of publication. From the outset, some companies anticipated limits on our freedom of access. Thus one specified at the outset that 'a suitable subject would concern the successful integration of coloured labour'. Another wanted access restricted to quite senior managers on the same issue. Only one company wrote formally that research 'will only be conducted with full company approval and the contents of your report and any subsequent publication will equally be agreed with the company and yourself.'

In practice, during the subsequent conduct of the research, additional oportunities or constraints sometimes arose. Thus some meetings were set up for us with shop stewards and workers, and with suppliers, local authorities and other bodies outside the companies. On one occasion, however, job design questions could not be studied in depth because other researchers had recently saturated the issue.

When it came to publication, two of the companies had already expressed a desire for anonymous treatment. A third was made anonymous rather than publish an agreed version in which they were named. The fourth company did not seek anonymity.

On those occasions when the cases were discussed with the firms, the main points of sensitivity related to internal audiences – how other managers, head office or the workforce, would react. Anonymity makes the case writer's task easier – inevitably an element of (we hope conscious) self-censorship arises when a firm is to be named – but we wanted a mixture of named and un-named firms for the sense of realism it gives.

Notes

Notes to Chapter 1: Private Solutions to Public Problems?

1. London Chamber of Commerce and Industry lunch, February 1981.
2. Ariah A. Ullmann, 'The Private Use of Public Interest: Formulating Strategies for the Political Environment', Working Paper 82–32, School of Management, State University of Binghampton (New York, 1982).
3. D. Votaw and S. Prakash Sethi (eds.), *The Corporate Dilemma: Traditional Values versus Contemporary Problems* (Englewood Cliffs, N.J.: Prentice-Hall, 1973) p. 10.
4. Edwin M. Epstein, 'The Social Role of Business Enterprise in Britain: an American Perspective – Part I', *Journal of Management Studies*, vol. 13, no. 3 (1976).
5. Richard Tanner Pascale and Anthony S. Athos, *The Art of Japanese Management* (Harmondsworth: Penguin Books, 1982).
6. William J. Conyngham, *The Modernisation of Soviet Industrial Management* (Cambridge University Press, 1982) p. 164.
7. Blair Ewing, 'The Good Goldfish: a Case Study in the Corporate Conscience', reprinted in Charles Perrow (ed.), *Organisational Analysis* (London: Tavistock, 1970).

Notes to Chapter 2: Managers: Good Goldfish?

1. Patrick Joyce, *Work, Society and Politics* (Brighton: Harvester, 1980).

2. Equally, the actions of the New Model Employers were regarded as indefensible (although for different reasons) by their preceding generation of small enterprises. See S. L. Smith, 'From Capitalist Domination to Urban Planning', paper presented to the *BSA/PSA Urban Politics/Urban History Study Group* (York, May 1981).

3. R. Dahrendorf, *Class and Class Conflict in Industrial Society* (London: Routledge & Kegan Paul, 1959).

4. J. K. Galbraith, *The New Industrial State* (Harmondsworth: Penguin Books, 1969).

5. A. A. Berle, *Power without Property* (New York: Harcourt Brace, 1960).

6. Charles Perrow (ed.), *Organisational Analysis* (London: Tavistock, 1970).

7. J. Scott, *Corporations, Classes and Capitalism* (London: Hutchinson, 1979).

8. Erik Olin Wright, 'Class Occupation and Organisation', in Dunkerley and Salaman (eds), *The International Yearbook of Organisation Studies 1979*.

9. Alan Berkeley Thomas, 'Managerial Careers and the Problems of Control', *Social Science Information*, vol. 22, no. 1 (1983) pp. 1–25.

10. Alvin W. Gouldner, *For Sociology* (London: Allen Lane, 1973).

11. Patrick Joyce, op. cit.

12. S. L. Smith, op. cit.

13. Derek Frazer, *Power and Authority in the Victorian City* (Oxford: Blackwell, 1979). Also, *Urban Politics in Victorian England* (Leicester University Press, 1976).

14. M. Heald, *The Social Responsibilities of Business Company and Community 1900–1960* (Cleveland and London: Case Western Reserve University, 1970).

15. A. G. Mileikovsky *et al.*, *Present-Day Non-Marxist Political Economy* (Moscow: Progress Publishers, 1981) pp. 351–68.

16. EIASM/EFMD, *Facing Realities: The Report of the European Societal Strategy Project* (Brussels, 1982).

Notes to Chapter 3: 'The Successful Integration of Foreign Labour'

1. The category 'foreign labour' was introduced in the 1940s to cover *all* immigrant labour, whether European, Asian or West

Indian. It is still used today. Today the vast majority within this category are black.

2. Amongst many here untold instances of this camaraderie was the case of the Indian worker who would dress up in drag and entertain his shop with a demonstration of castanet-dancing every Christmas.

3. In many Midlands foundries around the 1960s, the concentration of blacks in certain factories was seen as a threat, as they became militant through trade unions and the Indian Workers' Association. Many employers thus took advantage of the Racial Balance Clause in the 1968 Race Relations Act in an attempt to disperse black workers. At Harveys, the then personnel manager monitored the percentages of 'foreign labour' in each shop. The critical 51 per cent ratio was frequently exceeded, though no action was ever taken.

4. In the gang system, work was allocated to small 'gangs' of workers, who would between themselves determine the precise division of labour and the distribution of gang earnings.

5. There is, in fact, one exception. Despite management efforts, there are no blacks in maintenance.

Notes to Chapter 4: Treating the Outside World like the Weather

1. Mark Duffield, 'Capitalism and Labour Migration: the Case of Indians in the Foundry Industry', mimeo., Research Unit on Ethnic Relations (University of Aston, April 1982).

2. Young Enterprise Scheme (YES) is an educational charity which aims to bridge the gap between school and work by establishing mock companies among school-children, supervised by sponsoring companies.

3. We interviewed directors, personnel managers and public relations managers from the large manufacturers as well as certain key public officials. Significantly, the long-standing chairman of the largest company had only recently met for the first time the chairman of the third largest company.

Notes to Chapter 6: Mutuality of Benefits

1. An additional skilled setter-operator grade was also introduced later.
2. In addition, anyone considering setting up a small business in Melton Mowbray is offered, under MIDAS, free consultancy, financial advice and training in business management.
3. Petfoods has supported the findings of the Houghton Report which JACOPIS, under Lord Houghton, produced. It recommended a national dog-warden service funded on an increased dog licence fee. It was discussed in a Cabinet committee, but then the Labour government fell. Petfoods saw the report as encouraging responsible pet ownership.
4. Examples include 'Some Nutritional Differences between the Dog and the Cat', and 'Touching Pet Dogs and Changes in Blood Pressure'.
5. Diseases transmittable from animals to humans.
6. The proceedings of this symposium were published. See R. S. Anderson (ed.), *Pet Animals and Society* (London: Balliere Tindall, 1975). R. S. Anderson works at the Animal Studies Centre.

Notes to Chapter 7: Summary and Political Analysis of Case Studies

1. S. L. Smith, 'Corporations in Society: the Contribution of the Organisational Paradigms', *Business and Society Working Paper* (June 1982).
2. S. L. Smith, 'From Capitalist Domination to Urban Planning', paper presented to the 1983 Urban Change and Conflict Conference, Clacton, Essex.
3. D. Torrington, T. Hitner and D. Knights, *Management and the Multi-Racial Work Force* (Aldershot: Gower, 1982) p. 107.

Notes to Chapter 8: Managers and Corporate Social Policy

1. Emile Durkheim, *The Division of Labour in Society* (New York: Free Press, 1964).

167

2. Max Weber, *Economy and Society* (New York: Bedminster Press, 1968).
3. Karl Marx, *Capital*, vol. I (Moscow: Progress Publishers).
4. H. I. Ansoff, A. Edstrom and G. Hedland, 'Proposal for Research on Future Legitimacy (Role) of the Business Firm in Europe', European Institute for Advanced Studies in Management, Working Paper, 43 (Brussels, September 1978). Also, 'Facing Realities', *Report of European Societal Strategy Project* (EIASM/ EFMD, Brussels, 1982).

Notes to Appendix: Theory and Methods of Research

1. J. E. Post, 'Research into Business and Society', AACSB Conference (Berkeley, Calif., 26–31 July 1981).
2. For a review see R. J. Aldag and K. M. Bartol, 'Empirical Studies of Corporate Social Performance and Policy: a Survey of Problems and Results', in L. E. Preston (ed.), *Research in Corporate Social Performance and Policy*, vol. 1 (1978). A valuable exception is R. W. Ackerman, *The Social Challenge to Business* (Cambridge, Mass. and London: Harvard University Press, 1975).
3. J. E. Post, 'Research on Patterns of Corporate Response to Social Change', in L. E. Preston (ed.), *Research in Corporate Social Performance and Policy*, vol. 1 (1978) pp. 55–77; J. E. Post, op. cit. (1981); H. I. Ansoff, A. Edstrom and G. Hedland, 'Proposal for Research on Future Legitimacy (Role) of the Business Firm in Europe', EIASM Working Paper (1978); D. Votaw and S. P. Sethi (eds), *The Corporate Dilemma: Traditional Values versus Contemporary Problems* (Englewood Cliffs, N.J.: Prentice-Hall, 1973); M. Heald, *The Social Responsibilities of Business Company and Community 1900–1960* (Cleveland and London: Cave Western Reserve University, 1970); C. C. Walton, *Corporate and Social Responsibilities* (Belmont, Calif.: Wadsworth Publishing Co., 1967); E. A. Murray, 'The Corporate Public Affairs Function Report on a Large-Scale Research Project', AACSB Conference on Business Environmental/Public Policy (University of Maryland, 14 July 1980); E. M. Epstein, 'The Social Role of Business Enterprise in Britain: an American Perspective – Part II', *Journal of Management Studies*, vol. 14, no. 3 (October 1977) pp. 281–315; R. A. Bauer, 'The Corporate Response Process', in L. E. Preston

(ed.), *Research in Corporate Social Performance and Policy*, vol. 1 (1978) pp. 99–122.

4. P. L. Berger and T. Luckmann, *The Social Construction of Reality* (New York: Doubleday, 1966) p. 138.

5. B. Wilkinson, *The Shopfloor Politics of New Technology* (London: Heinemann, 1983).

6. R. J. Aldag and K. M. Bartol, op. cit. (1978).

7. R. W. Ackerman, op. cit. (1975).

8. See M. Poole, R. Mansfield, P. Blyton and P. Frost, *Managers in Focus* (Aldershot: Gower, 1981) p. 14.

9. See S. L. Smith, 'From Capitalist Domination to Urban Planning', BSA/PSA Urban Politics/Urban History Study Group Conference (University of York, May 1981).

10. See, for instance, R. M. Cyert and J. G. March, *A Behavioral Theory of the Firm* (Englewood Cliffs, N.J.: Prentice-Hall, 1963); J. Pfeffer, *Organisational Design* (Illinois: AHM Publishing, 1978); S. B. Bacharach and E. Lawler, *Power and Politics in Organisations* (San Francisco, Calif.: Jossey Bass, 1981); A. M. Pettigrew, *The Politics of Organisational Decision Making* (London: Tavistock, 1973) and 'On Studying Organisational Cultures', *Administrative Science Quarterly* (December 1979); S. Clegg, *The Theory of Power and Organisations* (London: Routledge & Kegan Paul, 1979).

Index

Index